Conversational ITALIAN for Travelers

Audio Dialogue Practice Book

Volume I, 2nd Edition

Kathryn Occhipinti

Stella Lucente

Conversational Italian for Travelers: Audio Dialogue Practice Book, Volume I, 2nd Edition

International Standard Book Number: 978-0-9903834-9-9
Publisher: Stella Lucente, LLC
Italian Editors: Maria Vanessa Colapinto and Simona Giuggioli
Graphics and Page Layout: Cyndi Clark
Cover Photograph: Kathryn Occhipinti
Entrance to Piazza San Marco, Venezia
Text Photographs: Kathryn Occhipinti
Rome,The Colosseum; Tivoli, Villa d'Este Gardens; Milan, Milano Centrale Railway Station; Milan, A view of modern downtown Milan from a rooftop garden; Milan, Duomo at Sunset

Order at:
Internet: www.Learntravelitalian.com or www.StellaLucente.com
Stella Lucente, LLC
P.O. Box 9640
Peoria, IL 61612

Introduction: How to Use This Book

Volumes 1 and 2 of the **Conversational Italian for Travelers Audio Dialogue Practice Book** are filled with useful phrases for the Italian student to read out loud. Essential Italian vocabulary and verb conjugation practice is provided, with examples that can be used in real-life situations. The English translation is given after each Italian phrase.

The **Audio Dialogue Practice Book**
was recorded with native Italian and English speakers
and is available for download
from Amazon.com and your favorite audio platform.

In each chapter of the Audio Dialogue Practice book, short Italian phrases are introduced first, and then included with exercises that focus on Italian verb conjugation. This method adds interest to the verb drills and allows for easy memorization of both frequently used Italian verbs and conversational phrases. As the chapter progresses, the phrases build into complex sentences. The more the example phrases are repeated, the more easily they are integrated into one's real-life Italian conversations and the more natural speaking in Italian becomes!

Both volumes of the **Audio Dialogue Practice Book** are companion books to the textbook **Conversational Italian for Travelers**, in that all content in Chapter 1 of the audio book is covered in Chapter 1 of the textbook, and so on, for each of the 18 chapters of the textbook. The audio book provides Italian language practice that includes and then goes beyond the examples provided in the textbook, to make conversational Italian truly come alive.

The focus of the **Conversational Italian for Travelers** textbook and the audiobook is on learning "all the Italian you need to enjoy your trip to Italy." The textbook is divided into three units: "Transportation," "City Life," and "At the Hotel and Restaurant." Volume 1of the **Audio Dialogue Practice Book** covers Chapters 1 through 9 of the textbook and includes the entire "Transportation" unit and the first half of the "City Life" unit. Volume 2 covers Chapters 10 through 18 and includes the second half of the "City Life" unit and the complete "At the Hotel and Restaurant" unit.

In Volume 1, the **Audio Dialogue Practice Book** introduces the Italian language with essential material for rote beginners, starting with the basics of conversation — easy meeting and greeting phrases. There is much repetition in the first two chapters of the names of countries and nationalities, which use Italian words that are similar to English and are easily understood by English speakers. In this way, the Italian student uses easy-to-learn Italian words to focus on understanding Italian masculine and feminine agreement and then ease into the more difficult concept of Italian verb conjugation. As the book progresses, additional vocabulary is gradually introduced, similar to how children learn their native language.

As the Volume 1 **Audio Dialogue Practice Book** progresses from beginning to intermediate material, Italian phrases are introduced that are useful for traveling throughout Italy on the train, in a taxi, or in an automobile. Counting and telling time in Italian is covered in the numbers section of the first six chapters. In other sections of the same chapters, this knowledge is applied to practical situations, such as negotiating when making a purchase or understanding the overhead announcements for train arrivals and departures. Chapters 1–7 emphasize the present tense Italian verbs used in every-day situations. In "City Life" Chapters 8 and 9, reflexive verbs and familiar commands are covered, so the Italian student can communicate feelings and actions with the friends they make while in Italy.

Volume 2 of the **Audio Dialogue Practice Book** covers material that is useful for the intermediate Italian student, including vocabulary that emphasizes social life and vacationing while in Italy; how to talk on the telephone, send an email, make reservations, and dine in an Italian restaurant is covered in detail. Verb practice includes describing likes/dislikes and speaking in the past, future, and conditional tenses.

Can the audio books be used without the **Conversational Italian for Travelers** textbook? For best results, it is recommended to read each chapter in the textbook first and learn the grammar behind the phrases in the audio books. The **Conversational Italian for Travelers** textbook was created specifically for adults who are motivated to learn Italian on their own. But for those Italian students who learn best by listening, whether learning on their own or in a formal Italian class, the audio material in both volumes of the **Audio Dialogue Practice Book** can stand alone as an invaluable learning aid. The topics covered in each exercise are summarized in a brief introduction, both in the books and in the audio recordings. One can just listen, listen, listen, and repeat to start speaking Italian immediately! Listen to each phrase once, or over and over again — as much or as little as needed, and follow the pace that is best for you!

Purchase **Conversational Italian for Travelers** audio books, download the audio, and start today to learn "all the Italian you need to enjoy your trip to Italy"! — *Kathryn Occhipinti*

Table of Contents

Conversational Italian for Travelers Audio Dialogue Practice Book

(Volume I, 2nd Edition)

Table of Contents

Table of Contents

Table of Contents

Table of Contents

Table of Contents

Table of Contents

Chapter 7 – A Family Reunion

Chapter 8 – Getting Ready

Table of Contents

Table of Contents

Table of Contents

Chapter 9 – It's a Party!

Chapter 1 – At the Airport

Practice – 1

Basic greetings

Buon giorno.	Good day.
Buon giorno.	Use for, "Good morning."
Buona giornata.	Use when an American would say: "Good afternoon,"or "Have a good day."
Buona sera.	Good evening.
Buona notte.	Good night.

Practice – 2

Basic greetings / Common expression city of origin **"Di dove?"** / Capital cities **(di)**

Buon giorno, signora.	Good morning, ma'am.
Di dov'è Lei?	Where are you from? (polite) (lit. From where are you?)
Sono di Londra.	(I) am from London.

Buon giorno, Maria.	Good afternoon, Mary.
Di dove sei?	Where are you from? (familiar)
Sono di Madrid.	(I) am from Madrid.

Buona sera, Maria.	Good evening, Mary.
Di dove sei?	Where are you from? (familiar)
Sono di Parigi.	(I) am from Paris.

Buona notte, Francesca.	Good night, Frances.
Buona notte, Laura.	Good night, Laura.

Practice – 3

Polite expressions of agreement

Si.	Yes.
Certo.	Of course.
D'accordo.	(I) agree.
Penso di si.	(I) think so.

Chapter 1 – At the Airport

Practice – 4

Polite expressions

Per favore.	Please.
Per piacere.	Please.
Grazie.	Thank you.
Molte grazie!	Thank you very much!
Tante grazie!	Many thanks!
Mille grazie!	Thanks a lot! (lit. A thousand thanks!)
Prego.	You're welcome.
Di niente!	You're welcome! (lit. It was nothing!)
Permesso?	May I (enter)?
Mi dispiace.	I'm sorry.
Mi scusi.	Excuse me. (polite command)
Scusa.	Excuse me. (familiar command)

Practice – 5

Polite expressions / Common expression city of origin **"Di dove?"** / Capital cities **(di)**

Per favore, signorina...	Please, miss...
Di dov'è Lei?	Where are you from? (polite)
Sono di Dublino.	(I) am from Dublin.

Per piacere, Maria...	Please, Mary...
Di dove sei?	Where are you from? (familiar)
Sono di Atene.	(I) am from Athens.

Permesso?	May I?
Di dove sei?	Where are you from? (familiar)
Sono di Berlino.	(I) am from Berlin.

Grazie, Maria.	Thank you, Mary.
Prego.	You are welcome.

Chapter 1 – At the Airport

Practice – 6

Basic greetings / Saying good bye

Ciao!	Hi! and Bye! (familiar)
Ciao bella!	Hi, beautiful (girl)!
Ciao bello!	Hi, handsome (boy)!
Come va?	How's it going?
Ci vediamo!	(Until) we see each other (again)!
Arrivederci!	Good bye! (familiar polite)
Arrivederla!	Good bye to you! (polite with respect)
A presto!	(See you) soon!
A dopo!	(See you) later!
A più tardi!	(A little) Later!

Practice – 7

Basic greetings

Chiamarsi – present tense **– mi chiamo, ti chiami, si chiama**

Common expression city of origin **"Di dove?"** / Capital cities **(di)**

Saying good bye

Buon giorno, signora. Come si chiama?	Good morning, ma'am. What is your name? (polite)
Mi chiamo Maria.	My name is Mary.
Di dov'è Lei?	Where are you from? (polite)
Sono di Mosca.	(I) am from Moscow.
Arrivederla.	Good bye to you. (polite with respect)

Ciao bella! Come ti chiami?	Hey, beautiful (girl)! What is your name? (familiar)
Mi chiamo Maria.	My name is Mary.
Di dove sei?	Where are you from? (familiar)
Sono del Cairo.	(I) am from Cairo.
Ci vediamo!	(Until) we see each other (again)!

Chapter 1 – At the Airport

Practice – 8

Common expression **"Dove?"** / Subject pronouns, questions and answers

Abitare – present tense **– abito, abiti, abita, abitiamo, abitate, abitano**

Countries **(in)**

Dove abito?	Where (do) (I) live?
Abito in Europa.	(I) live in Europe.

Dove abiti?	Where (do) (you) live? (familiar)
Abito in Italia.	(I) live in Italy.

Dove abita Lei?	Where (do) you live? (polite)
Abito in Irlanda.	(I) live in Ireland.

Dove abita lei?	Where (does) she live?
Abita in Spagna.	(She) lives in Spain.

Dove abita lui?	Where (does) he live?
Abita in Francia.	(He) lives in France.

Dove abitiamo?	Where (do) (we) live?
Abitiamo in Germania.	(We) live in Germany.

Dove abitate?	Where (do) (you all) live?
Abitiamo in Portogallo.	(We) live in Portugal.

Dove abitano?	Where (do) (they) live?
Abitano in Inghliterra.	(They) live in England.

Chapter 1 – At the Airport

Practice – 9

Basic greetings

Chiamarsi – present tense **– mi chiamo, ti chiami, si chiama**

Abitare – present tense **– abito, abiti, abita**

Common expression **"Dove?"** / Capital cities **(a)** / Saying good bye

Buon giorno! Come si chiama?	Good day! What is your name? (polite)
Mi chiamo Caterina.	My name is Kathy.
Dove abita Lei?	Where (do) you live? (polite)
Abito a Londra.	(I) live in London.
Arrivederla!	Good bye to you! (polite with respect)

Ciao bella! Come ti chiami?	Hi, beautiful (girl)! What is your name? (familiar)
Mi chiamo Rosa.	My name is Rose.
Dove abiti?	Where (do) (you) live? (familiar)
Abito a Parigi.	(I) live in Paris.
Ci vediamo!	(Until) we see each other (again)!

Ciao bella! Come va? Come ti chiami?	Hi, beautiful (girl)! How's it going? What is your name? (familiar)
Mi chiamo Laura.	My name is Laura.
Dove abiti?	Where (do) (you) live? (familiar)
Abito a Lisbona.	(I) live in Lisbon.
A presto!	(See you) soon!

Ciao! Come ti chiami?	Hi! What is your name? (familiar)
Mi chiamo Anna.	My name is Ann.
Dove abiti?	Where (do) (you) live? (familiar)
Abito a Dublino.	(I) live in Dublin.
A dopo!	(See you) later!

Chapter 1 – At the Airport

Practice – 10

Chiamarsi – present tense **– mi chiamo, ti chiami, si chiama**

Singular masculine forms of **bello/buono** / Names of people and countries

Come ti chiami?	What is your name? (familiar)
Mi chiamo Maria.	My name is Mary.
Che bel nome!	What a nice name!

Come si chiama?	What is your name? (polite)
Mi chiamo Caterina.	My name is Kathy.
Che bel nome!	What a beautiful name!

Come si chiama?	What is her name?
Si chiama Rosa.	Her name is Rose.
Che bel nome!	What a good name!

Come si chiama?	What is his name?
Si chiama Michele.	His name is Michael.
È un buon nome!	(It) is a good name!

Come si chiama?	What is its name?
Si chiama Europa.	Its name is Europe.
Che bel posto!	What a nice place!

Come si chiama?	What is its name?
Si chiama America.	It is called America.
È proprio un bel paese!	(It) is really a beautiful country!

Come si chiama?	What is its name?
Si chiama Italia.	It is called Italy.
È proprio un paese buono!	(It) is really a good country!

Chapter 1 – At the Airport

Practice – 11

Common expressions **"Dove?" "Ecco!"**

Vocabulary – At the airport

Caterina, dove sei?	Kathy, where are you?
Eccomi!	Here I am!

Dov'è l'uscita?	Where is the gate? (= exit to board the plane)
Eccola!	Here it is!

Dov'è la scala mobile?	Where is the escalator?
Eccola!	Here it is!

Pietro, dove sei?	Peter, where are you?
Eccomi!	Here I am!

Dov'è il bagaglio a mano?	Where is the carry on luggage?
Eccolo!	Here it is!

Dov'è la cintura di sicurezza?	Where is the seat belt?
Eccola!	Here it is!

Michele, dove sei?	Michael, where are you?
Eccomi!	Here I am!

Dov'è il biglietto aereo?	Where is the plane ticket?
Eccolo!	Here it is!

Dov'è la carta d'imbarco?	Where is the boarding pass?
Eccola!	Here it is!

Chapter 1 – At the Airport

Practice – 12

Common expressions **"Dove?" "Ecco!"**

Vocabulary – Countries with definite article – when identifying on a map

Caterina, dov'è l'Italia?	Kathy, where is (the country of) Italy?
Ecco l'Italia!	Here Italy is! (lit. Here is (the country of) Italy!)

Maria, dov'è l'America?	Mary, where is America?
Ecco l'America!	Here America is!

Michele, dove sono gli Stati Uniti d'America?	Michael, where is the United States of America?
Ecco gli Stati Uniti d'America!	Here is the United States of America!

Practice – 13

Numbers – Counting 1-10

Uno	1
Due	2
Tre	3
Quattro	4
Cinque	5
Sei	6
Sette	7
Otto	8
Nove	9
Dieci	10

Practice – 14

Numbers – Counting with **zero**

Zero	Zero
Uno zero	One zero
Due zeri	Two zeros
Dieci ha uno zero.	Ten has one zero.
Cento ha due zeri.	One hundred has two zeros.

Chapter 2 – At Customs in Italy

Practice – 1

Essere – present tense **– sono, sei, è, siamo, siete, sono**

Nationalities / Singular to plural

Io sono europeo.	I am European.
Tu sei inglese.	You are English. (familiar)
Lei è irlandese.	She is Irish.
Lui è spagnolo.	He is Spanish.

Noi siamo portoghesi.	We are Portuguese.
Voi siete francesi.	You all are French.
Loro sono tedeschi.	They are German.

Practice – 2

Essere – present tense **– sono, sei, è, siamo, siete, sono**

Nationalities / Capital cities **(di)** / Singular to plural

Io sono europea(o).	I am European. (female/male)
Tu sei inglese, di Londra.	You are English, from London. (familiar)
Lei è irlandese, di Dublino.	She is Irish, from Dublin.
Lui è spagnolo, di Madrid.	He is Spanish, from Madrid.

Noi siamo portoghesi, di Lisbona.	We are Portuguese, from Lisbon.
Voi siete francesi, di Parigi.	You all are French, from Paris.
Loro sono tedeschi, di Berlino.	They are German, from Berlin.

Chapter 2 – At Customs in Italy

Practice – 3

Essere – present tense **– io sono** / Countries with definite articles / Nationalities

Common expressions **"Da dove viene?" "Vengo dal, dall', dalla"**

Da dove viene?	Where are you from? (polite)
Vengo dall'Europa.	(I) come from Europe.
Io sono europeo(a).	I am European. (male/female)

Da dove viene?	Where are you from? (polite)
Vengo dall' Inghilterra.	(I) come from England.
Io sono inglese.	I am English.

Da dove viene?	Where are you from? (polite)
Vengo dall'Irlanda.	(I) come from Ireland.
Io sono irlandese.	I am Irish.

Da dove viene?	Where are you from? (polite)
Vengo dalla Spagna.	(I) come from Spain.
Io sono spagnolo(a).	I am Spanish. (male/female)

Da dove viene?	Where are you from? (polite)
Vengo dal Portogallo.	(I) come from Portugal.
Io sono portoghese.	I am Portuguese.

Da dove viene?	Where are you from? (polite)
Vengo dalla Francia.	(I) come from France.
Io sono francese.	I am French.

Da dove viene?	Where are you from? (polite)
Vengo dalla Germania.	(I) come from Germany.
Io sono tedesco(a).	I am German. (male/female)

Da dove viene?	Where are you from? (polite)
Vengo dalla Grecia.	(I) come from Greece.
Io sono greco(a).	I am Greek. (male/female)

Chapter 2 – At Customs in Italy

Practice – 3 (cont'd)

Essere – present tense **– io sono** / Countries with definite article / Nationalities

Common expressions **"Da dove viene?" "Vengo dal, dall', dalla"**

Da dove viene?	Where are you from? (polite)
Vengo dall'America (del nord).	(I) come from (North) America.
Io sono americana(o).	I am American. (female/male)

Da dove viene?	Where are you from? (polite)
Vengo dal Canada.	(I) come from Canada.
Io sono canadese.	I am Canadian.

Da dove viene?	Where are you from? (polite)
Vengo dal Messico.	(I) come from Mexico.
Io sono messicana(o).	I am Mexican. (female/male)

Da dove viene?	Where are you from? (polite)
Vengo dall'America del sud.	(I) come from South America.
Io sono sudamericana(o).	I am South American. (female/male)

Da dove viene?	Where are you from? (polite)
Vengo dalla Russia.	(I) come from Russia.
Io sono russa(o).	I am Russian. (female/male)

Da dove viene?	Where are you from? (polite)
Vengo dalla Cina.	(I) come from China.
Io sono cinese.	I am Chinese.

Chapter 2 – At Customs in Italy

Practice – 4

Andare – present tense (irreg.) **– vado, vai, va, andiamo, andate, vanno**

Countries **(in)**

Io vado in Italia.	I go to Italy.
Tu vai in Italia.	You go to Italy. (familiar)
Lei va in Italia.	She goes to Italy.
Lui va in Italia.	He goes to Italy.

Noi andiamo in Italia.	We go to Italy.
Voi andate in Italia.	You all go to Italy.
Loro vanno in Italia.	They go to Italy.

Practice – 5

Andare – present tense (irreg.) **– vado, vai, va, andiamo, andate, vanno**

Countries **(in)** / Days of the week

Io vado in Italia lunedì.	I go to Italy Monday.
Tu vai in Italia martedì.	You go to Italy Tuesday. (familiar)
Lei va in Italia mercoledì.	She goes to Italy Wednesday.
Lui va in Italia giovedì.	He goes to Italy Thursday.

Noi andiamo in Italia venerdì.	We go to Italy Friday.
Voi andate in Italia sabato.	You all go to Italy Saturday.
Loro vanno in Italia domenica.	They go to Italy Sunday.

Chapter 2 – At Customs in Italy

Practice – 6

Andare – present tense (irreg.) **– vado, vai, va, andiamo, andate, vanno**

Cities **(a)** / Days of the week with definite article for repetitive activity

Io vado a Milano il lunedì.	I go to Milan on Mondays. (= every Monday)
Tu vai a Milano il martedì.	You go to Milan on Tuesdays. (familiar)
Lei va a Milano il mercoledì.	She goes to Milan on Wednesdays.
Lui va a Milano il giovedì.	He goes to Milan on Thursdays.

Noi andiamo a Milano il venerdì.	We go to Milan on Fridays.
Voi andate a Milano il sabato.	You all go to Milan on Saturdays.
Loro vanno a Milano la domenica.	They go to Milan on Sundays.

Practice – 7

Andare – present tense (irreg.) **– vado, vai, va, andiamo, andate, vanno**

Cities **(a)** / Days of the week

Io vado a Milano oggi.	I go to Milan today.
Tu vai a Milano domani.	You go to Milan tomorrow. (familiar)
Lei va a Milano dopodomani.	She goes to Milan the day after tomorrow.
Lui va a Milano per tutta la giornata.	He goes to Milan for the entire day.

Noi andiamo a Milano ogni giorno.	We go to Milan every day.
Voi andate a Milano il fine settimana.	You all go to Milan (for) the weekend.
Loro vanno a Milano per sei giorni.	They go to Milan for six days.

Chapter 2 – At Customs in Italy

Practice – 8

Days of the week, questions and answers / Italian cities **(a)**

Essere – present tense **– è**

Andare – imperative and present tense (irreg.) **– Andiamo!**

Che giorno è oggi?	What day is today?
Oggi è lunedì.	Today is Monday.
Andiamo a Milano!	Let's go to Milan!

Che giorno è domani?	What day is tomorrow?
Domani è martedì.	Tomorrow is Tuesday.
Andiamo a Roma!	Let's go to Rome!

Che giorno è dopodomani?	What day is the day after tomorrow?
Dopodomani è mercoledì.	The day after tomorrow is Wednesday.
Andiamo a Firenze!	Let's go to Florence!

Che giorno è oggi?	What day is today?
Oggi è giovedì.	Today is Thursday.
Andiamo a Venezia!	Let's go to Venice!

Che giorno è domani?	What day is tomorrow?
Domani è venerdì.	Tomorrow is Friday.
Andiamo a Napoli!	Let's go to Naples!

Che giorno è dopodomani?	What day is the day after tomorrow?
Dopodomani è sabato.	The day after tomorrow is Saturday.
Andiamo a Palermo!	Let's go to Palermo!

Chapter 2 – At Customs in Italy

Practice – 9

Essere – present tense **– sono, sei, è, siamo, siete, sono**

Abitare – present tense **– abito, abiti, abita, abitiamo, abitate, abitano**

Andare – present tense (irreg.) **– vado, vai, va, andiamo, andate, vanno**

Tornare – present tense **– torno, torni, torna, torniamo, tornate, tornano**

Countries **(in)** / Nationalities / Months of the year **(a)** / Seasons **(in)** **(d')**

Io sono europea(o).	I am European. (female/male)
Io abito in Spagna.	I live in Spain.
Io vado in Italia a gennaio.	I go to Italy in January.
Io torno a febbraio.	I return in February.
Io torno d'inverno.	I return in the winter.

Tu sei europeo(a).	You are European. (male/female) (familiar)
Tu abiti in Francia.	You live in France. (familiar)
Tu vai in Italia a marzo.	You go to Italy in March. (familiar)
Tu torni ad aprile.	You return in April. (familiar)
Tu torni in primavera.	You return in the spring. (familiar)

Lei è europea.	She is European.
Lei abita in Germania.	She lives in Germany.
Lei va in Italia a maggio.	She goes to Italy in May.
Lei torna a giugno.	She returns in June.
Lei torna d'estate.	She returns in the summer.

Lui è europeo.	He is European.
Lui abita in Portogallo.	He lives in Portugal.
Lui va in Italia a luglio.	He goes to Italy in July.
Lui torna ad agosto.	He returns in August.
Lui torna d'estate.	He returns in the summer.

Chapter 2 – At Customs in Italy

Practice – 10

Essere – present tense – **sono, sei, è, siamo, siete, sono**
Abitare – present tense – **abito, abiti, abita, abitiamo, abitate, abitano**
Andare – present tense (irreg.) – **vado, vai, va, andiamo, andate, vanno**
Tornare – present tense – **torno, torni, torna, torniamo, tornate, tornano**
Countries **(in)** / Nationalities / Months of the year **(a)** / Singular to plural
Seasons **(in) (d')**

Noi siamo europei (europee).	We are Europeans. (europei = group of men or mixed group with men and women) (europee = group of women)
Noi abitiamo in Polonia.	We live in Poland.
Noi andiamo in Italia a settembre.	We go to Italy in September.
Noi torniamo a ottobre.	We return in October.
Noi torniamo in autunno.	We return in the fall.

Voi siete europei (europee).	You all are Europeans. (male/female groups)
Voi abitate in Belgio.	You all live in Belgium.
Voi andate in Italia a novembre.	You all go to Italy in November.
Voi tornate a dicembre.	You all return in December.
Voi tornate d'inverno.	You all return in the winter.

Loro sono europei (europee).	They are Europeans. (male/female groups)
Loro abitano in Svezia.	They live in Sweden.
Loro vanno in Italia a maggio.	They go to Italy in May.
Loro tornano a giugno.	They return in June.
Loro tornano d'estate.	They return in the summer.

Chapter 2 – At Customs in Italy

Practice – 11

Basic greetings / Common expression **"Come va?"** questions and answers

Saying good bye

Buon giorno, Maria. Come va?	Good morning, Maria. How's it going?
Va bene.	OK. (lit. It's going well.)
Bene. Arrivederci.	Good. (lit. It's fine.) Good bye.

Ciao, Caterina. Come va?	Hi, Kathy. How's it going?
Così, così.	So, so.
Mi dispiace. Ci vediamo.	I'm sorry. (Until) we see each other (again).

Ciao bella. Come va?	Hey, beautiful (girl). How's it going?
Non c'è male.	Not bad.
Bene. A dopo, bella!	Good. (See you) later, beautiful!

Buon giorno, Francesca. Come va?	Good day, Frances. How's it going?
Bene, grazie.	Well, thank you.
Bene. A presto!	Good. (lit. It's fine.) (See you) soon!

Ciao, Michele. Come va?	Hi, Michael. How's it going?
Molto male.	Very badly.
Mi dispiace. Ciao.	I'm sorry. Bye.

Ciao bella. Come va?	Hey, beautiful (girl). How's it going?
Abbastanza bene.	Pretty good.
Bene. Ci vediamo.	Good. We'll see each other (later).

Cosa vuole fare oggi?	What (do) (you) want to do today?
Andiamo a Milano!	Let's go to Milan!
Non mi va!	I don't feel like it! (idiomatic expression)

Chapter 2 – At Customs in Italy

Practice – 12

Parlare – present tense **– parlo, parli, parla, parliamo, parlate, parlano**

Important Phrases – Basic communication, **"Parla italiano?"**

Io parlo italiano.	I speak Italian.
Tu parli italiano.	You speak Italian. (familiar)
Lei parla italiano.	She speaks Italian.
Lui parla italiano.	He speaks Italian.

Noi parliamo italiano.	We speak Italian.
Voi parlate italiano.	You all speak Italian.
Loro parlano italiano.	They speak Italian.

Practice – 13

Parlare – present tense **– parlo, parli, parla, parliamo, parlate, parlano**

Important Phrases – Basic communication, **"Parla italiano?"**
questions and answers

Parla italiano?	(Do) (you) speak Italian? (polite)
Si, un po'.	Yes, a little bit.
Si, molto bene.	Yes, very well.
No, mi dispiace!	No, I'm sorry!

Parla inglese?	(Do) (you) speak English? (polite)
Si, parlo inglese.	Yes, (I) speak English.
No, parlo soltanto italiano.	No, (I) only speak Italian.
Dov'è un interprete?	Where is an interpreter?

Chapter 2 – At Customs in Italy

Practice – 14

Parlare – present tense **– parlo, parli, parla, parliamo, parlate, parlano**

Important Phrases – Basic communication, **"Può parlare...?"**

Può parlare più lentamente?	Could you speak more slowly?
Può parlare più piano?	Could you speak more slowly?
Può parlare più forte?	Could you speak more loudly?
Può parlare in inglese?	Could you speak in English?
Per favore, non parlare troppo veloce.	Please, do not speak too quickly.

Che cosa?	What?
Non ho sentito...	I didn't hear...
Non ho sentito che cosa hai detto.	I didn't hear what you said.
Non capisco...	I don't understand...
Non capisco che cosa hai detto.	I don't understand what you said.
Può ripetere?	Could you repeat (that)?

Practice – 15

Important Phrases – Basic communication, **"Come si dice..."** questions and answers

Vocabulary – At customs

Come si dice...?	How do you say...? (lit. How does one say...?)
...il passaporto?	...the passport?
...i documenti di viaggio?	...the travel documents?
...il visto (di ingresso)?	...the visa (of entry)?

Che cosa hai detto?	What did you say?
Come si dice in italiano?	How do you say (it) in Italian?
Come si chiama quello?	What is the name of that?
Cosa significa?	What does it mean?

Chapter 2 – At Customs in Italy

Practice – 16

Numbers – Counting 20-30

Venti	20
Ventuno	21
Ventidue	22
Ventitré	23
Ventiquattro	24
Venticinque	25
Ventisei	26
Ventisette	27
Ventotto	28
Ventinove	29
Trenta	30

Practice – 17

Numbers – Counting 30-40

Trenta	30
Trentuno	31
Trentadue	32
Trentatré	33
Trentaquattro	34
Trentacinque	35
Trentasei	36
Trentasette	37
Trentotto	38
Trentanove	39
Quaranta	40

Chapter 2 – At Customs in Italy

Practice – 18

Days of the week / Months of the year / Saying the date **(il numero di)**

Counting 2-10 and 20-31 / Ordinal number **primo**

Oggi è il due di gennaio.	Today is January 2nd.
Domani è il tre di gennaio.	Tomorrow is January 3rd.
Dopodomani è il quattro di gennaio.	The day after tomorrow is January 4th.

Oggi è il cinque di febbraio.	Today is February 5th.
Domani è il sei di febbraio.	Tomorrow is February 6th.
Dopodomani è il sette di febbraio.	The day after tomorrow is February 7th.

Oggi è l'otto di marzo.	Today is March 8th.
Domani è il nove di marzo.	Tomorrow is March 9th.
Dopodomani è il dieci di marzo.	The day after tomorrow is March 10th.

Oggi è il venti di aprile.	Today is April 20th.
Domani è il ventuno di aprile.	Tomorrow is April 21st.
Dopodomani è il ventidue di aprile.	The day after tomorrow is April 22nd.

Oggi è il ventitré di maggio.	Today is May 23rd.
Domani è il ventiquattro di maggio.	Tomorrow is May 24th.
Dopodomani è il venticinque di maggio.	The day after tomorrow is May 25th.

Oggi è il ventisei di giugno.	Today is June 26th.
Domani è il ventisette di giugno.	Tomorrow is June 27th.
Dopodomani è il ventotto di giugno.	The day after tomorrow June 28th.

Oggi è il ventinove di luglio.	Today is July 29th.
Domani è il trenta di luglio.	Tomorrow is July 30th.
Dopodomani è il trentuno di luglio.	The day after tomorrow is July 31st.
Oggi è il primo di agosto.	Today is August 1st. (Always use the ordinal number **primo** for the first of the month – see Chapter 3.)

Rome
The Colosseum

Chapter 3 – Taking a Taxi

Practice – 1

Avere – present tense **– ho, hai, ha, abbiamo, avete, hanno**

Expressions that use **avere – avere fame, avere sete** / The negative in Italian

Io ho fame.	I am hungry. (lit. I have hunger.)
Io non ho sete.	I am not thirsty. (lit. I do not have thirst.)

Tu hai fame.	You are hungry.
Tu non hai sete.	You are not thirsty.

Lei ha fame.	She is hungry.
Lei non ha sete.	She is not thirsty.

Lui ha fame.	He is hungry.
Lui non ha sete.	He is not thirsty.

Noi abbiamo fame.	We are hungry.
Noi non abbiamo sete.	We are not thirsty.

Voi avete fame?	Are you all hungry?
Voi non avete sete?	You all are not thirsty?

Loro hanno fame.	They are hungry.
Loro non hanno sete.	They are not thirsty.

Chapter 3 – Taking a Taxi

Practice – 2

Avere – present tense **– ho, hai, ha, abbiamo, avete, hanno**

Expressions that use **avere – avere fame, avere sete** / The negative in Italian

Common expressions vocabulary – replacing subject pronouns with girl, boy, or baby / Subject pronoun order for the **noi** form

Io ho fame.	I am hungry. (lit. I have hunger.)
Io non ho sete.	I am not thirsty. (lit. I do not have thirst.)

Tu hai fame.	You are hungry.
Tu non hai sete.	You are not thirsty.

La ragazza ha fame.	The girl is hungry.
Lei non ha sete.	She is not thirsty.

Il ragazzo ha fame.	The boy is hungry.
Lui non ha sete.	He is not thirsty.

Io e il bambino abbiamo fame.	I and the baby are hungry. (English = The baby and I are hungry.)
Noi non abbiamo sete.	We are not thirsty.

Tu e il bambino avete fame.	You and the baby are hungry.
Voi non avete sete.	You all are not thirsty.

Il ragazzo e la ragazza hanno fame.	The boy and girl are hungry.
Loro non hanno sete.	They are not thirsty.

Chapter 3 – Taking a Taxi

Practice – 3

Avere – present tense **– ho, hai, ha, abbiamo, avete, hanno**

Expressions that use **avere – avere caldo, avere freddo**

Essere – present tense – **È** for It is…

Months / The negative in Italian

Io ho freddo. È gennaio.	I am cold. (lit. I have cold.) (It) is January.
Io non ho caldo.	I am not hot. (lit. I do not have warmth.)

Tu hai freddo. È febbraio.	You are cold. (It) is February.
Tu non hai caldo.	You are not hot.

Lei ha freddo. È marzo.	She is cold. (It) is March.
Lei non ha caldo.	She is not hot.

Lui ha freddo. È inverno.	He is cold. (It) is wintertime.
Lui non ha caldo.	He is not hot.

Noi abbiamo caldo. È luglio.	We are hot. (It) is July.
Noi non abbiamo freddo.	We are not cold.

Voi avete caldo. È agosto.	You all are hot. (It) is August.
Voi non avete freddo.	You all are not cold.

Loro hanno caldo. È estate.	They are hot. (It) is summertime.
Loro non hanno freddo.	They are not cold.

Chapter 3 – Taking a Taxi

Practice – 4

Avere – present tense **– ho, hai, ha, abbiamo, avete, hanno**

Expressions that use **avere – avere freddo, avere caldo**

Essere – present tense – **È** for It is...

Months / The negative in Italian / Subject pronoun order for the **noi** form

Common expressions vocabulary – Replacing subject pronouns with lady, gentleman, young lady, woman, man

Io ho freddo. È settembre.	I am cold. (lit. I have cold.) (It) is September.
Io non ho caldo.	I am not hot. (lit. I do not have warmth.)

Tu hai freddo. È ottobre.	You are cold. (It) is October.
Tu non hai caldo.	You are not hot.

La signora ha freddo. È novembre.	The lady (married) is cold. (It) is November.
Lei non ha caldo.	She is not hot.

Il signore ha freddo. È autunno.	The gentleman is cold. (It) is autumn.
Lui non ha caldo.	He is not hot.

Io e la signorina abbiamo caldo. È aprile.	I and the young lady are hot. (English = The young lady and I are hot.) (It) is April.
Noi non abbiamo freddo.	We are not cold.

Tu e la donna avete caldo. È maggio.	You and the young woman are hot. (It) is May.
Voi non avete freddo.	You all are not cold.

L'uomo e la donna hanno caldo. È primavera.	The man and woman are hot. (It) is springtime.
Loro non hanno freddo.	They are not cold.

Chapter 3 – Taking a Taxi

Practice – 5

Avere – present tense **– ho, hai, ha, abbiamo, avete, hanno**

Expressions that use **avere** / **Essere –** present tense – **È** for It is…

Common expressions vocabulary – Replacing subject pronouns with **bimbo, bimba, fanciulla** / Subject pronoun order for the **noi** form

Io ho sonno.	I am sleepy. (lit. I have sleepiness.)
Tu hai bisogno di un letto.	You need a bed.
La fanciulla ha ragione.	The young girl is right (correct).
Il bimbo ha paura del buio.	The baby is afraid of the dark.

Io e il bimbo abbiamo sonno.	I and the baby are sleepy. (English = The baby and I are sleepy.)
Tu e il bimbo avete bisogno di un letto.	You and the baby need a bed.
La fanciulla e la sua bimba hanno fretta.	The young girl and her baby are in a hurry.

Practice – 6

Avere – present tense **– ho, hai, ha, abbiamo, avete, hanno**

Expressions that use **avere** / Important Phrases – Money

Cerco una banca.	(I) am looking (for) a bank.
Dov'è una banca?	Where is a bank?

Ho bisogno di cambiare i soldi.	(I) need to change (the) money.
Vorrei cambiare i soldi.	(I) would like to change (the) money.

Ho bisogno di cambiare i dollari con l'euro.	(I) need to change dollars for euros. (= the money in dollars for the money in euros)
Vorrei cambiare i dollari con l'euro.	(I) would like to change dollars for euros.

Qual è il tasso di cambio?	What is the exchange rate?
Qual è la tariffa?	What is the fee (for exchanging money)?
Qual è la percentuale?	What is the percentage?

Chapter 3 – Taking a Taxi

Practice – 7

Singular to plural nouns / Singular to plural **buono**

Common expressions vocabulary – Family

Il buon ragazzo	The good boy
I buoni ragazzi	The good boys

Il buon zio	The good uncle
I buoni zii	The good uncles

La buona ragazza	The good girl
Le buone ragazze	The good girls

Il ragazzo molto buono	The very good boy
I ragazzi molto buoni	The very good boys
La ragazza molto buona	The very good girl
Le ragazze molto buone	The very good girls

Practice – 8

Singular to plural nouns / Singular to plural **bello**

Common expressions vocabulary – Family

Il bel bambino	The nice baby
I bei bambini	The nice babies

Il bello zio	The handsome uncle
I begli zii	The handsome uncles

La bella donna	The beautiful woman
Le belle donne	The beautiful women

Il bambino molto bello	The very nice baby
I bambini molto belli	The very nice babies
La donna molto bella	The very beautiful woman
Le donne molto belle	The very beautiful women

Chapter 3 – Taking a Taxi

Practice – 9

Numbers – Counting 10-20

Dieci	10
Undici	11
Dodici	12
Tredici	13
Quattordici	14
Quindici	15
Sedici	16
Diciassette	17
Diciotto	18
Diciannove	19
Venti	20

Practice – 10

Costare – present tense **– (quanto) costa**

Important Phrases – Money (negotiating) / Numbers 15-20

Quanto costa?	How much (does it) cost?
Venti euro.	(It costs) 20 euros.
Troppo caro! Quindici euro, invece!	(That is) too expensive! 15 euros instead!
Non è in saldo... ma, diciannove va bene.	(It) is not on sale... but 19 is good.
No, è costoso! Forse diciassette?	No, (it) is expensive! Perhaps 17?
Diciotto. Non posso fare più sconto!	18. (I) can't discount it any more! (lit. I can't make it (any) more discounted!)
D'accordo.	Agreed.

Può pagare in contanti?	Can you pay in cash?
Mi può portare il resto?	Could you bring me the change?
Mi può dare la ricevuta, per favore?	Can you give me a receipt, please?

Chapter 3 – Taking a Taxi

Practice – 11

Costare – present tense **– Quanto costa?**

Vocabulary – Trains and automobiles / Important Phrases – Money (payments)

Numbers 10-16

Quanto costa il taxi?	How much is (the cost of) the taxi (ride)?
Il taxi costa dieci euro.	The taxi (ride) is (costs) 10 euros.

Quanto costa l'autobus?	How much is the bus (ride)?
L'autobus costa undici euro.	The bus costs 11 euros.

Quanto costa la metro? (= la metropolitana)	How much is the subway (ride)?
La metro costa dodici euro.	The subway costs 12 euros.

Quanto costa il vaporetto per il giorno?	How much is the (Venetian) passenger boat for the day?
Il vaporetto costa tredici euro.	The passenger boat costs 13 euros.

Quanto costa il biglietto?	How much is the ticket?
Il biglietto costa quattordici euro.	The ticket costs 14 euros.

Quanto costa il vagone letto?	How much is the sleeper car (on the train)?
Il vagone letto costa quindici euro.	The sleeper car costs 15 euros.

Quanto costa l'aliscafo?	How much is the hydrofoil (ride)?
L'aliscafo costa sedici euro.	The hydrofoil costs 16 euros.

Posso pagare con un assegno?	Can (I) pay with a check?
No, ma accettiamo la carta di credito.	No, but (we) accept credit cards.
Ma ho solamente il bancomat.	But I have only a debit card.
Documento, per favore.	Identification, please.
Posso pagare in contanti?	Can I pay in cash?
Ma, certo!	But, of course!

Chapter 3 – Taking a Taxi

Practice – 12

Common expression, **"Quanti anni ha?"** question and answers

Common expressions – Replacing subject pronouns according to age

Numbers 1, 10-50

Quanti anni ha il bimbo?	How old is the baby boy? (lit. How many years (does) the baby boy have?)
Il bimbo ha un anno.	The baby is one year old. (lit. has one year)

Quanti anni ha il ragazzino?	How old is the little boy?
Il ragazzino ha dieci anni.	The little boy is 10 years old.

Quanti anni ha la ragazzina?	How old is the little girl?
La ragazzina ha dieci anni.	The little girl is 10 years old.

Quanti anni ha il ragazzo?	How old is the boy?
Il ragazzo ha sedici anni.	The boy is 16 years old.

Quanti anni ha la ragazza?	How old is the girl?
La ragazza ha sedici anni.	The girl is 16 years old.

Quanti anni ha l'uomo?	How old is the man?
L'uomo ha trent'anni.	The man is 30 years old.

Quanti anni ha la donna?	How old is the woman?
La donna ha quarant'anni.	The woman is 40 years old.

Quanti anni ha il signore?	How old is the gentleman?
Il signore ha cinquant'anni.	The gentleman is 50 years old.

Quanti anni ha la signora?	How old is the lady?
La signora ha cinquantun'anni.	The lady is 51 years old.

Tivoli
Villa d'Este Gardens

Chapter 4 – At the Train Station

Practice – 1

Desiderare – present tense **– desidera** / **Volere –** conditional tense **– vorrei**

Vocabulary – At the train station / Italian cities / Use of **per** as to/for

Singular to plural **biglietto**

Buon giorno. Desidera?	Good day. What would (you) like? (polite)
Vorrei un biglietto di andata e ritorno per Milano.	(I) would like a round-trip ticket to/ for Milan. (lit. a ticket of going and returning)
Vorrei due biglietti di andata e ritorno per Roma.	(I) would like two round-trip tickets to/for Rome.

Buon giorno. Desidera?	Good morning. What would (you) like? (polite)
Vorrei un biglietto di sola andata per Firenze.	(I) would like a (one way) ticket to Florence.
Non ho bisogno di un biglietto di ritorno.	(I) don't need a return ticket.

Practice – 2

Volere – present tense (irreg.) **– voglio, vuoi, vuole,**
vogliamo, volete, vogliono

Vocabulary – At the train station / Italian cities / Use of **per** as to/for / Negative

Io voglio prendere il treno diretto per Milano.	I want to take the direct train to/for Milan.
Tu vuoi prendere l'interregionale per Milano.	You want to take the through train to/for Milan.
Lei vuole prendere l'espresso per Milano.	She wants to take the express train to/for Milan.

Noi non vogliamo fare il cambio.	We don't want to make a connection.
Voi non volete prendere il locale.	You all don't want to take the local train.
Loro non vogliono prendere il regionale.	They don't want to take the local train.

Chapter 4 – At the Train Station

Practice – 3

Vocabulary – At the train station / Italian cities / Ordinal numbers

Common expressions, **"Qual è?"** questions and answers

Qual è la prima fermata?	What is the first stop?
Qual è la seconda fermata?	What is the second stop?
Qual è la terza fermata?	What is the third stop?
Qual è la quarta fermata?	What is the fourth stop?
Qual è la quinta fermata?	What is the fifth stop?

La prima fermata è Milano.	The first stop is Milan.
La prossima fermata è Firenze.	The next stop is Florence.
L'ultima fermata è Roma.	The last stop is Rome.

Practice – 4

Dimenticare – present tense **– dimentico, dimentichi, dimentica di**

Dimenticare – past tense **– ha, abbiamo, avete, hanno dimenticato di**

Volere – present tense **– voglio** + infinitive

Timbrare / **Validare** / **Obliterare**

Vocabulary – At the train station / Negative / Singular to plural **biglietto**

Non voglio dimenticare di timbrare il biglietto.	(I) don't want to forget to stamp the ticket.
Non dimentichi di validare il biglietto.	Don't (you) forget to validate the ticket.
Lei non dimentica di obliterare (= timbrare) il biglietto.	She doesn't forget to cancel (= to stamp) the ticket.
Lui ha dimenticato di timbrare il biglietto.	He forgot to stamp the ticket.

Noi abbiamo dimenticato di timbrare i biglietti.	We forgot to stamp the tickets.
Voi avete dimenticato di validare i biglietti.	You all forgot to validate the tickets.
Loro hanno dimenticato di obliterare i biglietti.	They forgot to validate the tickets.

Chapter 4 – At the Train Station

Practice – 5

Cercare – present tense (irreg.) **– cerco, cerchi, cerca, cerchiamo, cercate, cercano**

Pagare – present tense (irreg.) **– pago, paghi, paga, paghiamo, pagate, pagano**

Vocabulary – At the train station / Italian cities / Numbers – Counting by 10's

Io pago un euro per il biglietto di andata a Torino.	I pay one euro for the ticket to/for Turin.
Io cerco la macchina obliteratrice.	I look for the ticket cancelling machine.

Tu paghi dieci euro per Genova.	You pay 10 euros to/for Genoa.
Tu cerchi il binario dodici.	You look for (the) track 12.

Lei paga venti euro per Venezia.	She pays 20 euros to/for Venice.
Lei cerca la carrozza letto.	She looks for the sleeper car.

Lui paga trenta euro per Firenze.	He pays 30 euros to/for Florence.
Lui cerca la carrozza ristorante.	He looks for the restaurant car.

Noi paghiamo quaranta euro per Napoli.	We pay 40 euros to/for Naples.
Noi cerchiamo la carrozza fumatori.	We look for the smoking car.

Voi pagate cinquanta euro per L'Aquila.	You all pay 50 euros to/for L'Aquila.
Voi cercate il biglietto veloce.	You all look for the automatic ticket dispenser.

Loro pagano sessanta euro per Palermo.	They pay 60 euros to/for Palermo.
Loro cercano il controllore.	They look for the ticket collector.

Chapter 4 – At the Train Station

Practice – 6

Important Phrases – Buying a ticket and taking the train

Numbers – Telling time

Vorrei un biglietto per Firenze.	(I) would like a ticket to Florence.
Vorrei il diretto.	(I) would like the through train.
Non vorrei cambiare treno.	(I) don't want to change trains.
Devo pagare il supplemento?	(Do) (I) have to pay an extra fee?

Vorrei un biglietto per Siena.	(I) would like a ticket to/for Siena.
Devo cambiare treno?	(Do) (I) have to change trains?
Quanto tempo c'è per la coincidenza?	How much time is there for the connection?
Dov'è l'orario?	Where is the train schedule?

A che ora parte il treno per Venezia?	At what hour (= when does) the train for Venice leave?
Parte alle sei.	(It) leaves at six. (6:00 AM)
Sta partendo.	(It) is leaving (right now).

A che ora arriva il treno per Pisa?	At what hour (= when does) the train for Pisa arrive?
Arriva alle diciotto.	(It) arrives at eighteen. (18:00 hours / 6:00 PM)
Sta arrivando.	(It) is arriving (right now).

È questo il treno per Bologna?	Is this the train for Bologna?
Prendo il treno alle otto.	(I) take the train at eight. (8:00 AM)
È questa la fermata per Bologna?	Is this the stop for Bologna?
È la prossima fermata per Bologna?	Is the next stop for Bologna?

Ho perso il treno!	(I) have missed the train!
Ho preso il treno sbagliato!	(I) have taken the wrong train!

Chapter 4 – At the Train Station

Practice – 7

Numbers – Telling time – **"Che ora è?" "Che ore sono?"** questions and answers

Numbers – 1-12

Che ora è?	What time is it? (lit. What hour is it?)
È l'una.	(It) is one (o'clock).
Che ore sono?	What time is it? (lit. How many hours are there?)
Sono le due.	It is 2 (o'clock). (lit. (The hours) are two.)
Sono le tre.	It is 3 (o'clock).
Sono le quattro.	It is 4 (o'clock).
Sono le cinque.	It is 5 (o'clock).
Sono le sei.	It is 6 (o'clock).
Sono le sette.	It is 7 (o'clock).
Sono le otto.	It is 8 (o'clock).
Sono le nove.	It is 9 (o'clock).
Sono le dieci.	It is 10 (o'clock).
Sono le undici.	It is 11 (o'clock).
Sono le dodici.	It is 12 (o'clock).

Practice – 8

Numbers – Telling time – Special expressions

Mezzanotte	Midnight
È mezzanotte.	(It) is midnight.
Mezzogiorno	Noon
È mezzogiorno.	(It) is noon.
Un quarto	A quarter (15 minutes)
Mezzo / Mezza	A half (30 minutes)
Tre quarti	Three quarters (45 minutes)

Di mattina	In the morning
Di pomeriggio	In the afternoon
Di sera	In the evening
Di notte	At night

Chapter 4 – At the Train Station

Practice – 9

Numbers – Telling time – Special expressions with singular/plural hours

Writing the time in Italian

È l'una.	(It) is one (o'clock).
È l'una e un quarto. (1,15)	(It) is a quarter past one. (1:15 AM)
È l'una e mezza. (1,30)	(It) is half past one. (1:30 AM)
È l'una e tre quarti. (1,45)	(It) is three quarters past one. (1:45 AM)

Sono le due.	(It) is two (o'clock).
Sono le due e un quarto. (2,15)	(It) is a quarter past two. (2:15 AM)
Sono le due e mezza. (2,30)	(It) is half past two. (2:30 AM)
Sono le due e tre quarti. (2,45)	(It) is three quarters past two. (2:45 AM)

È l'una di mattina.	(It) is one (o'clock) in the morning.
È l'una e un quarto di pomeriggio.	(It) is a quarter past one (o'clock) in the afternoon.
Sono le sei di sera.	(It) is six (o'clock) in the evening.
Sono le dieci di notte.	(It) is ten (o'clock) at night.

Practice – 10

Common expression **"Che cosa?"** / Vocabulary – At the train station

Numbers – Telling time with special expressions

Che cosa fai?	What are you doing?
Cosa c'è?	What's going on?
Cerco il binario dieci. Vado a Roma.	I am looking for track 10. I'm going to Rome.

Che cosa bisogna fare?	What (does one) need to do? (English = What do you need to do?)
Che si dice?	What should one say? (English = What does he/she/you (polite) say?)
Si dice, "Buon viaggio!"	One says, "Have a good trip!"

Chapter 4 – At the Train Station

Practice – 11

Volere – present tense (irreg.) **– voglio** + infinitive **"are"** verbs

Vocabulary – Chapters 1 – 4

Voglio viaggiare in Italia.	(I) want to travel to Italy.
Voglio andare a Milano e Roma.	(I) want to go to Milan and Rome.
Voglio iniziare oggi.	(I) want to start today.
Voglio cominciare oggi.	(I) want to start today.
Voglio tornare a maggio.	(I) want to return in May.

Voglio volare in aereo.	(I) want to fly in an airplane.
Voglio allacciare la cintura di sicurezza.	(I) want to fasten the seatbelt.
Voglio portare la mia valigia.	(I) want to bring my suitcase.
Non voglio dimenticare la mia valigia.	(I) don't want to forget my suitcase.

Voglio parlare italiano.	(I) want to speak Italian. (use for "in Italian")
Voglio imparare l'italiano.	(I) want to learn Italian. (use for "the Italian language")
Voglio studiare l'italiano.	(I) want to study Italian. (use for "the Italian language")
Voglio ricordare le parole italiane.	(I) want to remember the Italian words.
Non voglio dimenticare come parlare in italiano.	(I) don't want to forget how to speak in Italian.

Voglio comprare un biglietto.	(I) want to buy a ticket.
Voglio pagare per la seconda classe.	(I) want to pay for second class.
Voglio cercare l'orario.	(I) want to look for the schedule.
Voglio cambiare treno a Firenze.	(I) want to change train(s) at Florence.
Voglio la fermata a Pisa.	(I) want to stop at Pisa. (lit. I want the stop at Pisa.)

Milano Centrale Railway Station, Milan

Chapter 5 – On the Train to Milan

Practice – 1

Mangiare – present tense (irreg. spelling) **– mangio, mangi, mangia, mangiamo, mangiate, mangiano**

Possessive adjectives for family – singular, feminine

Io mangio la pizza.	I eat the pizza.
Tu mangi.	You eat.
Lei mangia. / Lui mangia.	She eats. / He eats.

Noi mangiamo la pizza.	We eat the pizza.
Voi mangiate.	You all eat.
Loro mangiano.	They eat.

Mia madre mangia gli spaghetti.	My mother eats the spaghetti. (= She eats the spaghetti.)
Tua madre mangia il formaggio.	Your mother eats the cheese.
Sua madre mangia il pane.	Her/His mother eats the bread.

Practice – 2

Studiare – present tense (irreg. spelling) **– studio, studi, studia, studiamo, studiate, studiano**

Possessive adjectives for family – singular, masculine

Definite article – with a language when used with **studiare**

Io studio l'italiano.	I study Italian. (= the Italian language)
Tu studi.	You study.
Lei studia. / Lui studia.	She studies. / He studies.

Noi studiamo l'italiano.	We study Italian.
Voi studiate.	You all study.
Loro studiano.	They study.

Mio padre studia l'italiano.	My father studies Italian. (= He studies Italian.)
Tuo padre studia il francese.	Your father studies French.
Suo padre studia lo spagnolo.	Her/His father studies Spanish.

Chapter 5 – On the Train to Milan

Practice – 3

Lasciare – present tense (irreg. spelling) **– lascio, lasci, lascia, lasciamo, lasciate, lasciano**

Possessive adjectives for family – singular, feminine

Io lascio…	I leave…
Tu lasci…	You leave…
Lei lascia… / Lui lascia…	She leaves… / He leaves…

Noi lasciamo…	We leave…
Voi lasciate…	You all leave…
Loro lasciano…	They leave…

Mia sorella lascia la campagna.	My sister leaves the countryside.
Tua sorella lascia Milano per sempre.	Your sister leaves Milan forever.
Sua sorella lascia il suo fidanzato.	Her/His sister leaves her boyfriend.

Practice – 4

Cominciare – present tense (irreg. spelling) **– comincio, cominci, comincia, cominciamo, cominciate, cominciano**

Iniziare – present tense (irreg. spelling) **– inizio, inizi, inizia, iniziamo, iniziate, iniziano**

Possessive adjectives for family – singular, masculine

Io comincio l'esame. / Io inizio l'esame.	I begin the exam.
Tu cominci. / Tu inizi.	You begin.
Lei comincia. / Lui inizia.	She begins. / He begins.

Noi cominciamo l'esame. Noi iniziamo l'esame.	We begin the exam.
Voi cominciate. / Voi iniziate.	You all begin.
Loro cominciano. / Loro iniziano.	They begin.

Mio fratello inizia l'esame.	My brother begins the exam. (= He begins the exam.)
Tuo fratello inizia.	Your brother begins.
Suo fratello inizia.	Her/His brother begins.

Chapter 5 – On the Train to Milan

Practice – 5

Abbracciare – present tense (irreg. spelling) **– abbraccio, abbracci, abbraccia abbracciamo, abbracciate, abbracciano**

Possessive adjectives for family – singular, with definite article for **famiglia, bambino**

Io abbraccio mia nonna.	I hug my grandmother.
Tu abbracci mia zia.	You hug my aunt.
Lei abbraccia sua figlia. Lui abbraccia sua figlia.	She hugs her daughter. He hugs his daughter.

Noi abbracciamo la nostra famiglia.	We hug our family.
Voi abbracciate la vostra famiglia.	You all hug your family.
Loro abbracciano la loro famiglia.	They hug their family.

Mio zio abbraccia mia cugina.	My uncle hugs my (female) cousin. (= He hugs my (female) cousin.)
Mia zia abbraccia mio cugino.	My aunt hugs my (male) cousin.
Mia mamma abbraccia la mia bambina.	My mother hugs my (female) baby.

Practice – 6

Baciare – present tense (irreg. spelling) **– bacio, baci, bacia, baciamo, baciate, baciano**

Possessive adjectives for family – singular, with definite article for **ragazzo(a), famiglia**

Io bacio il mio ragazzo.	I kiss my boyfriend.
Tu baci il tuo ragazzo.	You kiss your boyfriend.
Lei bacia il suo ragazzo.	She kisses her boyfriend.

Noi baciamo la nostra famiglia.	We kiss our family.
Voi baciate la vostra famiglia.	You all kiss your family.
Loro baciano la loro famiglia.	They kiss their family.

Mio padre bacia mia madre.	My father kisses my mother. (= He kisses my mother.)
Mio zio bacia mia zia.	My uncle kisses my aunt.
Mio nonno bacia mia nonna.	My grandfather kisses my grandmother.

Chapter 5 – On the Train to Milan

Practice – 7

Inviare – present tense (irreg. spelling) **– invio, invii, invia, inviamo, inviate, inviano**

Odiare – present tense (irreg. spelling) **– odio, odii, odia, odiamo, odiate, odiano**

Io invio la email. (= la posta elettronica)	I send the email.
Tu invii il fax.	You send the fax.
Lei invia l'SMS.	She sends the instant message.

Noi inviamo la lettera.	We send the letter.
Voi inviate le cartoline.	You all send the postcards.
Loro inviano il pacco.	They send the package.

Io odio la città.	I hate the city.
Tu odii il traffico.	You hate the traffic.
Lui odia il rumore.	He hates the noise.

Noi odiamo la campagna.	We hate the country.
Voi odiate lavorare.	You all hate to work.
Loro odiano studiare.	They hate to study.

Practice – 8

Vedere – present tense **– vedo, vedi, vede, vediamo, vedete, vedono**

Important Phrases – Asking for assistance

Io vedo l'albergo.	I see the hotel.
Tu vedi il ristorante.	You see the restaurant.
Lei vede la metro. (= la metropolitana)	She sees the subway.
Lui vede la stazione.	He sees the station.

Noi vediamo la fermata dell'autobus.	We see the bus stop.
Voi vedete la stazione dei treni.	You all see the train station.
Loro vedono la banca.	They see the bank.

Chapter 5 – On the Train to Milan

Practice – 9

Sapere – present tense (irreg.) **– so, sai, sa, sappiamo, sapete, sanno**

Important Phrases – Asking for assistance

Common expressions – **sapere**

Io so dov'è l'albergo.	I know where the hotel is.
Tu sai dov'è il ristorante.	You know where the restaurant is.
Lei sa dov'è il museo.	She knows where the museum is.
Lui sa dov'è l'ufficio postale.	He knows where the post office is.

Noi sappiamo dov'è la fermata.	We know where the stop is.
Voi sapete dov'è la banca.	You all know where the bank is.
Loro sanno dov'è la metro.	They know where the subway is.

Chi lo sa?	Who knows?
Lo so.	I know (it).
Non lo so.	I don't know (it).
Che io sappia...	As far as I know...
Lo sapevo!	I knew it!

Practice – 10

Conoscere – present tense **– conosco, conosci, conosce**
conosciamo, conoscete, conoscono

Possessive adjectives for family – singular, with definite article **la** for **famiglia**

Io conosco la tua famiglia.	I know your family.
Tu conosci la mia famiglia.	You know my family.
Lei conosce la sua famiglia.	She knows her family.
Lui conosce la sua famiglia.	He knows his family.

Noi conosciamo tuo padre.	We know your father.
Voi conoscete mia madre.	You all know my mother.
Loro conoscono mia zia.	They know my aunt.

Chapter 5 – On the Train to Milan

Practice – 11

Important Phrases – Asking for assistance, questions and answers

Using **in via** for street locations

Common expressions with **sapere**

Sapere – present tense (irreg.) **– so, sai, sa**

Lei sa dov'è il Grand Hotel?	(Do) you know where the Grand hotel is? (polite)
Si, lo so. È in via Grande.	Yes, (I) know (it). (It) is on Grand Street.

Sai dov'è il ristorante Mirabella?	(Do) (you) know where the restaurant Mirabella is? (familiar)
Mi dispiace; non lo so.	I'm sorry; (I) don't know (it).

Scusi, mi può dire dov'è la stazione dei treni?	Excuse me, (can) (you) tell me where the train station is? (polite)
No, non lo so.	No, (I) don't know (it).

Mi sai dire dov'è la fermata dell'autobus?	(Can) (you) tell me where the bus stop is? (familiar)
La fermata dell'autobus è in via Verde.	The bus stop is on Green Street.

Lei sa quando arriva il treno?	(Do) you know when the train arrives? (polite)
Il treno arriva alle sette.	The train arrives at seven (o'clock).

Scusi, mi può dire quando arriva il treno?	Excuse me, could (you) tell me when the train arrives? (polite)
Il treno arriva alle otto.	The train arrives at eight (o'clock).

Scusi, mi può dire quando parte il treno?	Excuse me, could (you) tell me when the train leaves? (polite)
Il treno parte alle sei.	The train leaves at six (o'clock).

Chapter 5 – On the Train to Milan

Practice – 12

Vedere – present tense (irreg.) **– vedo, vedi, vede, vediamo, vedete, vedono**

Vocabulary – In the country / Colors

Io vedo la collina verde.	I see the green hill.
Tu vedi il fiore giallo.	You see the yellow flower.
Lei vede il masso grigio.	She sees the gray rock.
Lui vede il cielo blu.	He sees the blue sky.

Noi vediamo il maiale rosa.	We see the pink pig.
Voi vedete il cavallo marrone.	You all see the brown horse.
Loro vedono la mucca bianca e nera.	They see the white and black cow.

Practice – 13

Numbers – More telling time, from 8:45-9:00 / Counting by fives
Writing the time in Italian

Che ore sono?	What time is it?
Sono le otto e quarantacinque. (8,45)	It is 8:45 AM.
Sono le nove meno un quarto. (8,45)	It is a quarter to 9. (It is 15 minutes to 9.) (8:45 AM)

Sono le otto e cinquanta. (8,50)	It is 8:50 AM.
Sono le nove meno dieci. (8,50)	It is 10 minutes to 9. (8:50 AM)

Sono le otto e cinquantacinque. (8,55)	It is 8:55 AM.
Sono le nove meno cinque. (8,55)	It is 5 minutes to 9:00. (8:55 AM)

Sono le nove. (9,00)	It is 9.00 AM.

Chapter 5 – On the Train to Milan

Practice – 14

Numbers – More telling time, **"A che ora?"** / 24 hour clock

A che ora arriva l'aereoplano?	What time (does) the airplane arrive?
A mezzogiorno.	At noon.

A che ora parte il treno?	What time (does) the train leave?
All'una.	At one (o'clock). (1:00 AM)
Alle tredici.	At 13:00 (hours). (1:00 PM)

A che ora comincia il viaggio?	At what time (does) the trip start?
Alle sette.	At seven (o'clock). (7:00 AM)
Alle diciannove.	At 19:00 (hours). (7:00 PM.)

A che ora inizia il film?	At what time (does) the movie begin?
Alle ventuno.	At 21:00 (hours). (9:00 PM)

A che ora finisce il film?	At what time (does) the movie end?
A mezzanotte.	At midnight.

A che ora apre il museo?	At what time (does) the museum open?
Alle dieci.	At ten (o'clock). (10:00 AM)

A che ora chiude il museo?	At what time (does) the museum close?
Alle venti.	At 20:00 (hours). (8:00 PM)

Chapter 6 – Driving with Pietro

Practice – 1

Forming sentences with **essere** + **bravo**

Caterina è una brava ragazza.	Kathy is a good girl. (talented)
Caterina è brava.	Kathy is good. (talented)

Pietro è un bravo ragazzo.	Peter is a good boy. (talented)
Pietro è bravo.	Peter is good. (talented)

Caterina e Francesca sono brave ragazze.	Kathy and Frances are good girls.
Caterina e Francesca sono brave.	Kathy and Frances are good.

Pietro e Michele sono bravi ragazzi.	Peter and Michael are good boys.
Pietro e Michele sono bravi.	Peter and Michael are good.

Pietro e Francesca sono bravi genitori.	Peter and Frances are good parents.
Pietro e Francesca sono bravi.	Peter and Frances are good.

Practice – 2

Forming sentences with **vecchio, cattivo, grande, nuova** – adjective placement

Pietro è un vecchio amico.	Peter is an old (longstanding) friend.
Caterina è un'amica vecchia / anziana.	Kathy is a friend (who is) old / elderly.

Pietro è un uomo cattivo.	Peter is a bad (not helpful / not nice) man.
Caterina è una cattiva donna.	Kathy is a mean woman.

Michele è diventato grande.	Michael has grown up. (= become big)
Pietro è un grande uomo.	Peter is a great man.

Questa è una macchina nuova.	This is a (brand) new car.
Questa è una nuova macchina.	This is a different car.

Chapter 6 – Driving with Pietro

Practice – 3

Important Phrases – Renting a car

Dov'è l'autonoleggio?	Where is the rental car place?
Vorrei noleggiare una macchina.	(I) would like to rent a car.

Che modelli avete?	What models do (you all) have?
Vorrei una macchina piccola.	(I) would like a small car.

Avete una macchina più piccola?	(Do) (you all) have a smaller car?
Avete una macchina più grande?	(Do) (you all) have a bigger car?

Non vorrei il cambio manuale.	(I) don't want a manual shift.
Voglio il cambio automatico.	(I) want an automatic shift.

Quanto costa al giorno? (= Quanto costa per un giorno?)	What does (it) cost for the day?
Quanto costa per una settimana?	What does (it) cost for a week?
Quanto costa per il fine settimana?	What does (it) cost for the weekend?

È tutto compreso?	Is everything included?
È compresa l'assicurazione?	Is the insurance included?
È compresa la benzina?	Is the gas included?
C'è l'imposta IVA? (IVA = imposta sul valore aggiunto)	Is there an IVA tax? (IVA = value added tax)

Practice – 4

Vocabulary – At the gas station

Dov'è la stazione di servizio?	Where is the service/gas station?
Può fare il pieno, per favore?	Could you fill it up (with gas), please?
Può controllare l'olio, per favore?	Could you check the oil, please?
Può controllare l'acqua, per favore?	Could you check the water, please?
Ho una gomma a terra.	(I) have a flat tire.
Può cambiare la gomma, per favore?	Could you change the tire, please?
Può caricare la batteria, per favore?	Could you charge the battery, please?

Chapter 6 – Driving with Pietro

Practice – 5

Vocabulary – Parking signs and important road signs

Passo carrabile	No parking (pass by) driveway
Divieto di sosta	Forbidden stopping (= no parking)
Divieto di accesso	Forbidden entry (= no access)
Area pedonale	Pedestrian zone
Senso unico	One-way street
Senso vietato	Forbidden street (= no entry)
Anabbaglianti sempre accesi	Headlights always on
Dare la precedenza	Give way / Yield

Practice – 6

Important Phrases – Asking for transportation assistance

Mi può chiamare un taxi per favore?	Could you call a taxi for me, please?
Mi può portare in via Grande, per favore?	Could you take me to Grand Street, please?
Vorrei prendere il treno.	I would like to take the train.
C'è una stazione della metro vicino?	Is there a subway station (stop) near-by?
Dammi le chiavi della macchina!	Give me the car keys! (familiar command)

Practice – 7

Important Phrases – Getting in and out of vehicles

Sali in macchina!	Get in the car! (familiar command)
Scendi dalla macchina!	Get out of the car! (familiar command)
Salgo sull'autobus.	I get on the bus.
Scendi dall'autobus!	Get off the bus! (familiar command)
Salgo sul treno.	I get on the train.
Scendi dal treno!	Get off the train! (familiar command)
Salgo sull'aereo.	I get on the plane.
Scendi dall'aereo!	Get off the plane! (familiar command)

Chapter 6 – Driving with Pietro

Practice – 8

Leggere – present tense (irreg. pronunciation) **– leggo, leggi, legge, leggiamo, leggete, leggono**

Vocabulary – Driving in the city

Io leggo il cartello.	I read the traffic sign.
Tu leggi.	You read.
Lei legge.	She reads.

Noi leggiamo il cartello.	We read the traffic sign.
Voi leggete.	You all read.
Loro leggono.	They read.

Practice – 9

Leggere – present tense (irreg. pronunciation) **– legge**

Possessive adjectives – singular, feminine

Vocabulary – Driving in the city

La mia amica legge il cartello.	My (female) friend reads the traffic sign. (= She reads the traffic sign.)
La tua amica legge.	Your friend reads.
La sua amica legge.	Her friend reads.

La nostra amica legge il cartello.	Our friend reads the traffic sign.
La vostra amica legge.	Your friend reads.
La loro amica legge.	Their friend reads.

Chapter 6 – Driving with Pietro

Practice – 10

Spingere – present tense (irreg. pronunciation) **– spingo, spingi, spinge, spingiamo, spingete, spingono**

Io spingo la porta chiusa.	I push the door closed.
Tu spingi.	You push.
Lui spinge.	He pushes.

Noi spingiamo la porta chiusa.	We push the door closed.
Voi spingete.	You all push.
Loro spingono.	They push.

Practice – 11

Spingere – present tense (irreg. pronunciation) **– spinge**

Possessive adjectives – singular, masculine

Il mio amico spinge la porta chiusa.	My (male) friend pushes the door closed. (= He pushes the door closed.)
Il tuo amico spinge.	Your friend pushes.
Il suo amico spinge.	His friend pushes.

Il nostro amico spinge la porta chiusa.	Our friend pushes the door closed.
Il vostro amico spinge.	Your friend pushes.
Il loro amico spinge.	Their friend pushes.

Chapter 6 – Driving with Pietro

Practice – 12

Cucinare – present tense **– cucino, cucini, cucina, cuciniamo, cucinate, cucinano**

Cuocere – present tense (irreg. spelling) **cuoce, cuociono**

Io cucino il pollo.	I cook the chicken.
Tu cucini l'agnello.	You cook the lamb.
Lei cucini la salsa di pomodoro.	She cooks the tomato sauce.
La salsa di pomodoro cuoce in pentola.	The tomato sauce cooks (heats up) in a pot.

Noi cuciamo la bistecca.	We cook the steak.
Voi cucinate il pesce.	You all cook the fish.
Loro cucinano gli spaghetti.	They cook the spaghetti.
Gli spaghetti cuociono sul fornello.	The spaghetti cooks (heats up) on the stove.

Practice – 13

Cucinare – present tense **– cucinano**

Possessive adjectives – plural, feminine

Le mie amiche cucinano la colazione per i bambini.	My (female) friends cook (the) breakfast for the children.
Le tue amiche cucinano il pranzo stasera.	Your friends cook (the) dinner tonight.
Le sue amiche cucinano una cena meravigliosa.	Her friends cook a wonderful dinner.

Le nostre amiche cucinano tutto il giorno per la festa.	Our friends cook all day for the party.
Le vostre amiche cucinano la specialità della casa.	Your friends cook the specialty of the house.
Le loro amiche cucinano gli spaghetti alla bolognese.	Their friends cook Spaghetti Bolognese.

Chapter 6 – Driving with Pietro

Practice – 14

Vincere – present tense (irreg. pronunciation) **– vinco, vinci, vince, vinciamo, vincete, vincono**

Important Phrases – Money

Numbers – Counting 10 – 60 by tens

Io vinco dieci euro.	I win 10 euros.
Tu vinci venti euro.	You win 20 euros.
Lui vince trenta euro.	He wins 30 euros.

Noi vinciamo quaranta euro.	We win 40 euros.
Voi vincete cinquanta euro.	You all win 50 euros.
Loro vincono sessanta euro.	They win 60 euros.

Practice – 15

Vincere – present tense (irreg. pronounciation) **– vincono**

Possessive adjectives – plural, masculine

Important Phrases – Money / Irreg plural **amici**

I miei amici vincono cento euro.	My friends win one hundred euros. (= They win one hundred euros.)
I tuoi amici vincono.	Your friends win.
I suoi amici vincono.	His friends win.

I nostri amici vincono cento euro.	Our friends win one hundred euros.
I vostri amici vincono.	Your friends win.
I loro amici vincono.	Their friends win.

Chapter 6 – Driving with Pietro

Practice – 16

Bere – present tense (irreg.) **– bevo, bevi, beve, beviamo, bevete, bevono**

Possessive adjectives – singular and plural things, masculine

Io bevo il mio bicchiere di vino.	I drink my glass of wine.
Tu bevi il tuo bicchiere d'acqua.	You drink your glass of water.
Lui beve il suo bicchiere di latte.	He drinks his glass of milk.

Noi beviamo i nostri bicchieri di vino.	We drink our glasses of wine.
Voi bevete i vostri bicchieri d'acqua.	You all drink your glasses of water.
Loro bevono i loro bicchieri di latte.	They drink their glasses of milk.

Practice – 17

Scegliere – present tense (irreg.) **– scelgo, scegli, sceglie, scegliamo, scegliete, scelgono**

Possessive adjectives – singular and plural things, feminine

Io scelgo la mia macchina all'autonoleggio.	I choose my car at the auto rental place.
Tu scegli la tua macchina.	You choose your car.
Lei sceglie la sua macchina.	She chooses her/his car.

Noi scegliamo le nostre macchine.	We choose our cars.
Voi scegliete le vostre macchine.	You all choose your cars.
Loro scelgono le loro macchine.	They choose their cars.

Chapter 6 – Driving with Pietro

Practice – 18

Spegnere – present tense (irreg.) **– spengo, spegni, spegne, spegniamo, spegnete, spengono**

Vocabulary – Driving in the city / Turning off lights and electronics

Io spengo i fari.	I turn off the headlights.
Tu spegni la luce.	You turn off the light.
Lui spegne la macchina.	He turns off the car.

Noi spegniamo la TV.	We turn off the TV.
Voi spegnete la radio.	You all turn off the radio.
Loro spengono i computer.	They turn off the computers.

Practice – 19

Accendere – present tense **– accendo, accendi, accende, accendiamo, accendete, accendono**

Vocabulary – Driving in the city / Turning on lights and electronics

Io accendo gli anabbaglianti.	I turn on the headlights.
Tu accendi le luci.	You turn on the lights.
Lei accende la macchina.	She starts the car.

Noi accendiamo la TV.	We turn on the TV.
Voi accendete la radio.	You all turn on the radio.
Loro accendono i computer.	They turn on the computers.

Chapter 6 – Driving with Pietro

Practice – 20

Stare – present tense (irreg.) **– sto, stai, sta, stiamo, state, stanno**

Stare bene / Stare male

Stai buono! vs. **Sei buono!**

Common expressions with **bene**

Io sto bene.	I am feeling well.
Tu stai molto bene.	You are feeling really well.
Lei sta abbastanza bene.	She is well enough.

Noi stiamo male.	We are not feeling well. (lit. We are feeling badly.)
Voi state male?	You all are not feeling well?
Loro stanno male.	They are not feeling well.

Stai buono!	Be good! (familiar command to a male)
Stai buona!	Be good! (familiar command to a female)
Sei buono!	You are good! (familiar to a male)
Sei buona!	You are good! (familiar to a female)

Practice – 21

Stare – present tense (irreg.) **– sto, stai, sta, stiamo, state, stanno**

Stare fermo / Stare zitto!

Io sto fermo. / Io sto ferma.	I keep still. (male/female speaker)
Tu stai fermo. / Tu stai ferma.	You keep still. (to a male/to a female)
Stai zitto! Stai zitta!	Keep quiet! (to a male) Keep quiet! (to a female) (English = Shut up!)
Lei sta ferma. / Lui sta fermo.	She keeps still. / He keeps still.

Noi stiamo fermi.	We keep still.
Voi state fermi.	You all keep still.
State zitti!	You all shut up!
Loro stanno fermi.	They keep still.

Chapter 6 – Driving with Pietro

Practice – 22

Stare – present tense (irreg.) **– sto, stai, sta, stiamo, state, stanno**

Present progressive tense **– stare + ando** for **"are"** verbs

Uses of **stare + preparando**

Io sto preparando la valigia.	I am packing the suitcase.
Tu stai preparando la colazione.	You are making breakfast.
Lei sta preparando la cena.	She is making dinner.

Noi stiamo preparando una torta.	We are making a cake.
Voi state preparando una festa a sorpresa per Maria.	You all are making a surprise party for Mary.
Loro stanno preparando la camera per gli ospiti.	They are getting the room ready for the guests.

Practice – 23

Stare – present tense (irreg.) **– sto, stai, sta, stiamo, state, stanno**

Present progressive tense **– stare + endo** for **"ere"** verbs

Bere – present progressive tense (irreg. gerund) **– bevendo**

Io sto leggendo il cartello.	I am reading the traffic sign.
Tu stai spingendo la porta aperta.	You are pushing the door open.
Lui sta vincendo il gioco.	He is winning the game.

Noi stiamo leggendo il libro.	We are reading the book.
Voi state bevendo il vino.	You all are drinking the wine.
Loro stanno scegliendo bene.	They are choosing well.

Chapter 6 – Driving with Pietro

Practice – 24

Volere – present tense (irreg.) **– voglio, vuoi**

Amare – present tense **– amo, ami**

Common expressions, **"Volere bene"** questions and answers

Mi vuoi bene?	Do you care for me?
Si, ti voglio bene.	Yes, I care for you.

Figlia mia, mi vuoi bene?	My daughter, do you love me?
Ma, certo mamma! Ti voglio bene!	But, of course, mom! I love you!

Papà, mi vuoi bene?	Dad, do you love me?
Si, ti voglio bene.	Yes, I love you.

Mi ami, Michele mio?	Do you love me, my Michael?
Si, ti amo, Francesca, mia cara moglie.	Yes, I love you, Frances, my dear wife.

Michele, è il nostro primo anniversario. Mi ami ancora oggi?	Michael, it is our first anniversary. Do you still love me today?
Si, ti amo oggi e per sempre.	Yes, I love you today and forever.

Caterina, ho una brutta notizia.	Kathy, I have bad news.
Che notizia, amore mio?	What news, my love?
Non ti voglio più bene.	I don't love you any more.
Ma, perché?	But, why?
Non lo so. Mi dispiace!	I don't know. I'm sorry!

Chapter 7 – A Family Reunion

Practice – 1

Vocabulary – Use of different forms of **benvenuto**

Possessives with **a casa**

Ciao, Michele!	Hi, Michael!
Benvenuto a casa mia!	Welcome to my house!

Caterina, mia cara!	Kathy, my dear!
Benvenuta a casa mia!	Welcome to my house!

Buona sera, signor e signora Manzini.	Good evening, Mr. and Mrs. Manzini.
Benvenuti a casa nostra!	Welcome to our house!

Buon giorno, Francesca e Caterina!	Good day, Frances and Kathy!
Benvenute a casa nostra!	Welcome to our house!

Practice – 2

Dormire – present tense **– dormo, dormi, dorme, dormiamo, dormite, dormono**

Dormire – present progressive tense **– stare + endo** for **"ire"** verbs

Vocabulary – At home

Io dormo a casa.	I sleep at home.
Tu dormi in camera da letto.	You sleep in the bedroom.
Lui dorme con la finestra aperta.	He sleeps with the window open.

Noi dormiamo ogni giorno per la siesta.	We sleep every day for the siesta.
Voi dormite per un paio di ore.	You all sleep for a couple of hours.
Loro dormono bene la domenica.	They sleep well on Sundays.

Io sto dormendo.	I am sleeping. (= falling asleep)
Tu stai dormendo?	Are you sleeping?
Lui sta dormendo fino a tardi oggi.	He is sleeping (until) late today.

Chapter 7 – A Family Reunion

Practice – 3

Aprire – present tense **– apro, apri, apre, apriamo, aprite, aprono**

Numbers – More telling time / Vocabulary – At home

Io apro la porta.	I open the door.
Tu, apri la porta!	You, open the door! (familiar command)
A che ora apre il museo?	What time (does) the museum open?

Noi apriamo le finestre.	We open the windows.
Voi aprite le persiane.	You all open the shutters.
Loro aprono il camino per l'inverno.	They open (up) the fireplace for winter.

Practice – 4

Partire – present tense **– parto, parti, parte, partiamo, partite, partono**

Partire – present progressive tense **– stare + endo** for **"ire"** verbs

Numbers – More telling time / Vocabulary – At the train station

Io parto per Milano.	I leave for Milan.
Tu parti presto con il treno.	You leave soon on the train.
A che ora parte il treno?	What time does the train leave?

Noi partiamo lunedì per il viaggio.	We leave (on) Monday for the trip.
Voi partite per la campagna domenica.	You all leave for the country (on) Sunday.
Loro partono per la città stasera.	They leave for the city tonight.

Io sto partendo.	I am leaving (right now).
Tu stai partendo?	Are you leaving (right now)?
Il treno sta partendo per Roma.	The train is leaving for Rome (right now).

Chapter 7 – A Family Reunion

Practice – 5

Finire – present tense (irreg.) **– finisco, finisci, finisce, finiamo, finite, finiscono**

Numbers – More telling time / Vocabulary – At home

Io finisco la scuola alle tre ogni giorno.	I finish school at three every day.
Tu finisci il lavoro alle sei.	You finish work at six.
A che ora finisce il film?	What time does the film finish?

Noi finiamo stasera alle otto.	We finish tonight at eight.
Voi finite la cena e poi ci vediamo.	You all finish dinner and then we'll see each other.
Loro finiscono di fare tante cose per i bambini.	They finish making many things for the children.

Practice – 6

Capire – present tense (irreg.) **– capisco, capisci, capisce, capiamo, capite, capiscono**

Adverbs of quantity

Io capisco parecchio d'italiano.	I understand a good deal of Italian.
Tu capisci molte cose.	You understand many things.
Lei non capisce niente di me.	She understands nothing about me.

Noi capiamo poco della storia.	We understand a little of the history.
Voi capite troppo.	You all understand too much.
Loro capiscono abbastanza bene.	They understand pretty well.

Chapter 7 – A Family Reunion

Practice – 7

Dire – present tense (irreg.) **– dico, dici, dice, diciamo, dite, dicono**

Important phrases – Basic communication

Dico di, "Si."	I say, "Yes."
Dici di, "No."	You say, "No."
Come si dice?	How does one say (it)? (polite) (English = How do you say it?)

Noi diciamo che è vero.	We say that it is true.
Voi dite tante cose.	You all say many things.
Loro dicono che è buono.	They say it is good.

Practice – 8

Salire – present tense (irreg.) **– salgo, sali, sale, saliamo, salite, salgono**

Important Phrases – Getting in vehicles and going up stairs

Io salgo in macchina.	I get in the car.
Tu sali sul treno.	You get on the train.
Lui sale sulla bicicletta.	He gets on the bicycle.

Noi saliamo sull'autobus.	We get on the bus.
Voi salite sull'aereo.	You all get on the airplane.
Loro salgono le scale.	They go up the stairs.

Chapter 7 – A Family Reunion

Practice – 9

Uscire – present tense (irreg.) **– esco, esci, esce, usciamo, uscite, escono**

Uscire – present progressive tense **– stare + endo** for **"ire"** verbs

Important phrases – Coming and going

Io esco presto stamattina.	I go out early this morning.
Tu esci alle otto oggi?	Do you go out at eight today?
Lei esce il fine settimana con Michele.	She goes out on the weekend with Michael.

Noi usciamo dal ristorante.	We go out from the restaurant.
Voi uscite dal cinema.	You all go out from the cinema.
Loro escono dal museo.	They go out from the museum.

Io sto uscendo.	I am going out (right now).
Tu stai uscendo?	Are you going out (right now)?
Lei sta uscendo con Michele.	She is going out (right now) with Michael.

Practice – 10

Venire – present tense (irreg.) **– vengo, vieni, viene, veniamo, venite, vengono**

Venire – present progressive tense **– stare + endo** for **"ire"** verbs

Important Phrases – Coming and going

Io vengo a casa.	I come home.
Vengo io!	I'm coming!
Vieni qua!	You come here! (familiar command)
Michele, vieni qua!	Michael, you come here! (command)
Caterina viene in chiesa la domenica.	Kathy comes to church on Sundays.

Noi veniamo a casa tua oggi per cena.	We (will) come to your house today for dinner.
Voi venite a casa mia oggi.	You all (will) come to my house today.
Loro vengono per le feste.	They (will) come for the holidays.

Io sto venendo a casa tua.	I am coming to your house (right now).
Tu stai venendo?	Are you coming (right now)?
Lei sta venendo.	She is coming (right now).

Chapter 7 – A Family Reunion

Practice – 11

Venire – present tense (irreg.) **– vengo, vieni** / **Uscire –** present tense (irreg.)

Volere – present tense (irreg.) **– voglio**

Important Phrases – Coming and going / Negative – **Non voglio**

Non voglio venire a casa presto.	I don't want to come home early.
Non voglio uscire stasera.	I don't want to go out tonight.
Non voglio uscire per cena stasera.	I don't want to go out for dinner tonight.
Non voglio uscire con Francesca.	I don't want to go out with Frances.

Io vengo a casa.	I come home.
Vengo io!	I'm coming!
Michele, vieni qua!	Michael, come here! (familiar command)

Practice – 12

Andare – present tense (irreg.) **– vado, vai, va, andiamo, andate, vanno**

Venire – present tense (irreg.) **– viene, vengono**

Vocabulary – **"andare a trovare" "venire a trovare"**

Possessive / Italian relatives

Io vado a trovare mia nonna.	I go to visit my grandmother.
Mia nipote viene a trovarmi oggi.	My granddaughter comes to visit me today.

Tu vai a trovare tua cugina.	You go to visit your cousin.
Mia cugina viene a trovarmi oggi.	My cousin comes to visit me today.

Lui va a trovare la sua fidanzata.	He goes to visit his fiancée.
Il suo fidanzato viene a trovarla oggi.	Her fiancé comes to visit her today.

Noi andiamo a trovare i nostri genitori.	We go to visit our parents.
I nostri figli vengono a trovarci oggi.	Our children come to visit us today.

Voi andate a trovare i vostri parenti.	You all go to visit your relatives.
I nostri parenti vengono a trovarci oggi.	Our relatives come to visit us today.

Chapter 7 – A Family Reunion

Practice – 13

Adverbs of quantity

Niente	Nothing
Io ho niente da fare oggi.	I have nothing to do today.

Poco	A little
Io ho poco denaro.	I have a little money.
Un po' di	A little bit of
Vorrei un po' di spaghetti.	I would like a little bit of spaghetti.

Abbastanza	Enough of
Abbastanza bene	Pretty well / Pretty good
Abbastanza buono	Good enough
Abbastanza presto	Soon enough
Non abbastanza bravo	Not good enough
Abbastanza grande	Large enough
Abbastanza poco	Small enough

Parecchio	A lot of / A good deal of
Un sacco di	A lot of (lit. a sac of)
Ho un sacco di soldi. (= ho molti soldi)	I have a lot of money. (idiomatic expression: lit. I have a sack of money.)

Molto / Tanto	Much / A lot
Ho molto da fare oggi.	I have a lot to do today.
Troppo	Too much
Ho troppo da fare oggi.	I have too much to do today.

Chapter 7 – A Family Reunion

Practice – 14

Numbers – Counting 100-900 by hundreds

Cento	100
Duecento	200
Trecento	300
Quattrocento	400
Cinquecento	500
Seicento	600
Settecento	700
Ottocento	800
Novecento	900

Practice – 15

Numbers – Counting 100-200 by tens

Cento	100
Centodieci	110
Centoventi	120
Centotrenta	130
Centoquaranta	140
Centocinquanta	150
Centosessanta	160
Centosettanta	170
Centottanta	180
Centonovanta	190
Duecento	200

Chapter 7 – A Family Reunion

Practice – 16

Numbers – Counting 200-300 by tens

Duecento	200
Duecentodieci	210
Duecentoventi	220
Duecentotrenta	230
Duecentoquaranta	240
Duecentocinquanta	250
Duecentosessanta	260
Duecentosettanta	270
Duecentottanta	280
Duecentonovanta	290
Trecento	300

Practice – 17

Numbers – Counting 220-230 by ones

Duecentoventi	220
Duecentoventuno	221
Duecentoventidue	222
Duecentoventitré	223
Duecentoventiquattro	224
Duecentoventicinque	225
Duecentoventisei	226
Duecentoventisette	227
Duecentoventotto	228
Duecentoventinove	229
Duecentotrenta	230

Chapter 7 – A Family Reunion

Practice – 18

Common expressions with **essere** + **di** + infinitive verb

Ricorda di prendere la medicina.	Remember to take the medicine.
Sono sicuro di ricordare questo posto.	I am sure to remember this place.

Sono contento di stare qui.	I am happy to stay here.
Sono felice di incontrare mio cugino oggi.	I am happy to meet my cousin today.

Sono fortunato di mangiare questa cena.	I am fortunate to (be able to) eat this dinner.
Sono libero di viaggiare.	I am free to travel.
Sono stanco di volare.	I am tired of flying.

Practice – 19

Common expressions with **essere** + **di** + infinitive verb / Telling a story

Caterina è libera di viaggiare in Europa.	Kathy is free to travel in Europe.
Ma, è stanca di volare.	But, she is tired of flying.
Lei è contenta di stare qui, a Milano, con i suoi nuovi amici.	She is happy to stay here, in Milan, with her new friends.
Ci sono tante brave persone al Grand Hotel.	There are so many good people at the Grand Hotel.
Dice Caterina, "Sono sicura di ricordare questo posto per sempre!"	Kathy says, "I am sure to remember this place forever!"

Chapter 7 – A Family Reunion

Practice – 20

Verbs which take **di** + infinitive verb

Dice di stare bene.	She says she is well.
Finisco di lavorare per oggi.	I finish working for today.
Penso di partire alle tre.	I think of leaving at three.
Spero di trovare i soldi.	I hope to find the money.
Decido di guidare con attenzione.	I decide to drive attentively.
Aspetto di ricevere un regalo.	I wait to receive a present.
Cerca di studiare bene.	Try to study well.
Ricorda di prendere la medicina.	Remember to take the medicine.
Non dimenticare di prendere la medicina!	Don't forget to get the medicine! (familiar command)

Practice – 21

Verbs which take **di** + infinitive verb / Telling a story – **"Pensa all'amore…"**

Oggi, Francesca pensa all'amore.	Today, Frances thinks of love.
Lei aspetta il ritorno a casa di suo marito, Pietro.	She waits for the return home of her husband, Peter.
Pietro parla d'amore a lei ogni sera.	Peter speaks of love to her every evening.
E oggi, è il compleanno di Pietro.	And, today, it is Peter's birthday.
Ma, per ora, Francesca finisce di lavorare.	But, for now, Frances finishes working.
Per prima cosa, Francesca pulisce la casa.	At first, Frances cleans the house.
Secondo, Francesca prepara la cena.	Second, Frances makes the dinner.
E poi, lei si ricorda di prendere la torta.	And then, she remembers to get the cake.
Finalmente, Francesca cerca di trovare i migliori piatti per la tavola.	Finally, Frances tries to find the best plates for the table.
Aspetta che arrivano i parenti, e finalmente Pietro alle sette.	She waits for the relatives to arrive, and finally Peter at 7:00.
È una bella sorpresa per lui!	It is a wonderful surprise for him!

Milan

A view of modern downtown Milan from a rooftop garden.

Chapter 8 – Getting Ready

Practice – 1

Divertirsi – present tense **– mi diverto, ti diverti, si diverte, ci divertiamo, vi divertite, si divertono**

Io mi diverto.	I enjoy myself.
Tu ti diverti.	You enjoy yourself.
Lei si diverte.	She enjoys herself.
Lui si diverte.	He enjoys himself.

Noi ci divertiamo.	We enjoy ourselves.
Voi vi divertite.	You all enjoy yourselves.
Loro si divertono.	They enjoy themselves.

Practice – 2

Alzarsi – present tense **– mi alzo, ti alzi, si alza, ci alziamo, vi alzate, si alzano**

Io mi alzo.	I get up. (lit. I get myself up.)
Tu ti alzi.	You get up.
Lei si alza.	She gets up.
Lui si alza.	He gets up.

Noi ci alziamo.	We get up.
Voi vi alzate.	You all get up.
Loro si alzano.	They get up.

Chapter 8 – Getting Ready

Practice – 3

Alzarsi – present tense **– mi alzo, ti alzi, si alza**

Svegliarsi – present tense (irreg. spelling) **– mi sveglio, ti svegli, si sveglia**

Important Phrases – Getting ready

Mi sveglio.	I wake up. (lit. I wake myself up.)
Mi alzo.	I get up. (lit. I get myself up.)
Mi alzo presto.	I get up early.
Mi alzo alle sei.	I get up at 6 AM.
Mi alzo tardi domani.	I (am going to) get up late tomorrow.
Chiamami alle nove, per favore.	Call me at nine (o'clock), please.

Ti svegli.	You wake up.
Ti alzi.	You get up.
Ti alzi presto.	You get up early.
Ti alzi alle sei.	You get up at 6 AM.
Ti alzi tardi domani.	You (are going to) get up late tomorrow.

Si sveglia.	She/He wakes up.
Si alza.	She/He gets up.
Si alza presto.	She/He gets up early.
Si alza alle sei.	She/He gets up at 6 AM.
Si alza tardi domani.	She/He (is going to) get up late tomorrow.

Chapter 8 – Getting Ready

Practice – 3 (cont'd)

Alzarsi – present tense **– ci alziamo, vi alzate, si alzano**

Svegliarsi – present tense (irreg. spelling) **– ci svegliamo, vi svegliate, si svegliano**

Important Phrases – Getting ready

Ci svegliamo.	We wake up.
Ci alziamo tra un paio d'ore.	We get up in a couple of hours.
Ci alziamo un po' più tardi.	We get up a little later. (lit. a little more late)
Il sabato ci alziamo più tardi.	On Saturdays, we get up later. (lit. more late)

Vi svegliate.	You all wake up.
Vi alzate tra un paio d'ore.	You all get up in a couple of hours.
Vi alzate un po' più tardi.	You all get up a little later.
Il sabato, vi alzate più tardi.	On Saturdays, you all get up later.

Loro si svegliano.	They wake up.
Loro si alzano tra un paio d'ore.	They get up in a couple of hours.
Loro si alzano un po' più tardi.	They get up a little later.
Il sabato, loro si alzano più tardi.	On Saturdays, they get up later.

Practice – 4

Sedersi – present tense (irreg.) **– mi siedo, ti siedi, si siede,**
ci sediamo, vi sedete, si siedono

Io mi siedo.	I sit down. (lit. I sit myself down.)
Tu ti siedi.	You sit down.
Lei si siede.	She sits down.
Lui si siede.	He sits down.

Noi ci sediamo.	We sit down.
Voi vi sedete.	You all sit down.
Loro si siedono.	They sit down.

Chapter 8 – Getting Ready

Practice – 5

Direct reflexive verbs – present tense – first person singular:
bagnarsi,farsi, lavarsi, asciugarsi, pettinarsi, prepararsi, vestirsi, mettersi, truccarsi

Important Phrases – Getting ready

Mi faccio il bagno. Faccio un bagno.	I take a bath. (lit. I make myself the bath.)
Mi faccio il doccia. Faccio una doccia.	I take a shower. (lit. I make myself the shower.)
Mi lavo.	I wash myself.
Mi asciugo.	I dry myself off.
Mi pettino.	I comb my hair.
Mi preparo per il lavoro.	I get (myself) ready for work.
Mi vesto.	I get dressed. (lit. I dress myself.)
Mi metto i vestiti.	I put on my clothes. (lit. I put on myself the clothes.)
Mi trucco. / Mi faccio la barba.	I put on my make-up. / I shave.
Mi metto la giacca e le scarpe.	I put on my jacket and my shoes.
Vado al lavoro. / Vado a lavorare.	I go to work.

Practice – 6

Direct reflexive verbs – present tense – first person singular:
spogliarsi, svestirsi, mettersi, rilassare, riposarsi, addormentarsi

Important Phrases – Getting ready

Torno a casa.	I return home.
Alle nove, mi spoglio.	At 9 PM, I get undressed. (lit. I undress myself.)
Mi tolgo le scarpe.	I take off my shoes.
Mi metto il pigiama e le ciabatte.	I put on my pajamas and slippers.
Mi rilasso.	I relax (myself).
Alle dieci e mezzo, ho sonno.	At 10:30, I'm sleepy.
Dico a mia figlia: "A nanna! Buona notte!"	I say to my daughter: "It is night-night! Good night!"
Mi riposo.	I rest (myself).
Mi addormento.	I fall (myself) asleep.

Chapter 8 – Getting Ready

Practice – 7

Important Phrases – Getting ready, questions and answers

Buon giorno! Hai dormito bene?	Good morning! Did you sleep well?
Si, molto bene, grazie.	Yes, very well, thank you.
Si, ho dormito molto bene, grazie.	Yes, I slept very well, thank you.
Vuoi un caffè?	(Do) you want a (cup of) coffee?
Si, vorrei un caffè.	Yes, I would like a coffee.
Si, vorrei del caffè.	Yes, I would like some coffee.
Vuoi del tè?	(Do) you want a (cup of) tea?
Si, vorrei un tè.	Yes, I would like a (cup of) tea.
No, vorrei un bicchiere di acqua.	No, I would like a glass of water.
Vorrei un bicchiere di succo d'arancia.	I would like a glass of orange juice.

Practice – 8

Reflexive and non-reflexive verb forms that change in meaning: **chiamarsi, sentirsi, lavarsi, mettersi, prepararsi**

Io chiamo mia zia Maria al telefono.	I call my aunt Mary on the telephone.
Mi chiamo Caterina.	I call myself Kathy. (English = My name is Kathy.)

Io sento le campane della chiesa.	I hear the church bells.
Mi sento bene.	I feel (myself) well.

Io lavo l'automobile.	I wash the car.
Mi lavo ogni mattina.	I wash myself every morning.

Io metto i piatti sul tavolo.	I put the plates on the table.
Mi metto il vestito.	I put on (myself) the dress. (English = I put on my dress.)

Io preparo la cena.	I make the dinner.
Mi preparo per uscire.	I get (myself) ready to go out.

Chapter 8 – Getting Ready

Practice – 9

Reflexive and non-reflexive verb forms that change in meaning:
occuparsi, provarsi, spostarsi, informarsi

La famiglia occupa un posto importante nella storia.	The family occupies an important place in history.
Mi occupo di fare la cena.	I am taking care of making the dinner.

Prova gli spaghetti!	Try the spaghetti!
Mi provo questo vestito.	I try on (myself) this dress.

Sposto la mia macchina dall'altra parte della strada.	I move my car across the street.
Mi sposto facilmente.	I move myself easily.

Io informo gli studenti sull' esame.	I inform the students about the test.
Mi informo sul viaggio a Milano.	I inquire about traveling to Milan.

Practice – 10

Reciprocal reflexive verbs:
abbracciarsi, amarsi, baciarsi, fidanzarsi, incontrarsi, salutarsi, sposarsi, telefonarsi, vedersi

Si abbracciano e si baciano.	They hug and kiss each other.
Pietro e Francesca si amano.	Peter and Frances love each other. (= romantic love)
I miei amici si fidanzano.	My friends get engaged to each other.
Si sposano domenica.	They marry (each other) Sunday. They get married.
Pietro e Caterina si vogliono bene.	Peter and Kathy care about each other very much.
Caterina e zia Rosa si salutano.	Kathy and Aunt Rose greet each other.

Ci vediamo al teatro.	We (will) see each other at the theater.
Ci telefoniamo domani.	We (will) call each other tomorrow.
Ci vogliamo bene.	We care about each other very much.

Chapter 8 – Getting Ready

Practice – 11

Infinitive reflexive verbs and reflexive pronouns – first person singular

Volere – present tense (irreg.) **– voglio**

Voglio divertirmi.	I want to enjoy myself.
Voglio riposarmi.	I want to rest (myself).
Voglio alzarmi.	I want to get (myself) up.

Practice – 12

Reflexive verbs and the use of **si** to make impersonal statements

Come si dice…?	How does one say…?
In Italia, si parla italiano.	In Italy, one speaks Italian.
In America, si parlano molte lingue.	In America, they speak many languages. (= many languages are spoken)

Practice – 13

Common expressions with **"andare a trovare"** and **"venire a trovare"**

Io vado a trovare nonna oggi.	I go to visit grandma today.
Tu vai a trovare zia Rosa.	You go to visit Aunt Rose.
Mia sorella va a trovare mamma.	My sister goes to visit mom.

Noi andiamo a trovare i nostri genitori a Milano.	We go to visit our parents in Milan.
Voi venite a trovare la famiglia.	You all come to visit the family.
I nostri figli vengono a trovarci.	Our children come to visit us.

Chapter 8 – Getting Ready

Practice – 14

Forming adverbs of manner – **"o"** changes to **"a" + mente**

Corretto	Correct
Correttamente	Correctly
Lei studia correttamente.	She studies correctly.
Perfetto	Perfect
Perfettamente	Perfectly
Lei legge l'italiano perfettamente.	She reads Italian perfectly.
Vero	True
Veramente	Truly
Venezia è una città veramente bella.	Venice is a truly beautiful city.

Practice – 15

Forming adverbs of manner – drop **"e" + mente** / keep **"e" + mente**

Speciale	Special
Specialmente	Especially
Lei è una ragazza specialmente bella.	She is an especially beautiful girl.
Facile	Easy
Facilmente	Easily
Lei parla italiano facilmente.	She speaks Italian easily.
Regolare	Regular
Regolarmente	Regularly
Lei parla italiano regolarmente.	She speaks Italian regularly.
Breve	Brief
Brevemente	Briefly
Lui parla brevemente.	He speaks briefly.
Frequente	Frequent
Frequentemente	Frequently
Io vado a Roma frequentemente.	I go to Rome frequently.
Paziente	Patient
Pazientemente	Patiently
Lui aspetta pazientemente.	He waits patiently.
Veloce	Quick
Velocemente	Quickly
Lui corre velocemente.	He runs quickly.

Chapter 8 – Getting Ready

Practice – 16

Common expressions with **trovare**

Cerco di trovare la strada giusta.	I must try to find the right road.
Trovo il film divertente.	I find the film amusing.
Devo trovare un modo per vederti.	I must find a way to see you.
Trova conforto in Dio.	Take comfort in God.

Devo trovare la risposta.	I must try to find the answer.
Devo trovare la soluzione.	I must try to find the solution.
È necessario trovare il tempo per studiare.	It is necessary to find the time to study.

Troviamoci dopo cena.	Let's meet each other after dinner.
Non mi trovo bene con Maria.	I don't get on well with Maria.
Dove si trova il ristorante?	Where is the restaurant located?
Il ristorante si trova in via Grande.	The restaurant is on Grand Street.

Practice – 17

Numbers – Counting 1,000 -10,000 by thousands

Mille	1,000
Duemila	2,000
Tremila	3,000
Quattromila	4,000
Cinquemila	5,000
Seimila	6,000
Settemila	7,000
Ottomila	8,000
Novemila	9,000
Diecimila	10,000

Chapter 8 – Getting Ready

Practice – 18

Numbers – Counting 100,000-1,000,000 by hundred thousands

Centomila	100,000
Duecentomila	200,000
Trecentomila	300,000
Quattrocentomila	400,000
Cinquecentomila	500,000
Seicentomila	600,000
Settecentomila	700,000
Ottocentomila	800,000
Novecentomila	900,000
Un millione	1,000,000

Practice – 19

Numbers – Use of **mille, cento, un migliaio** and **una migliaia**

Il dipinto costa cento dollari.	The painting costs one hundred dollars.
Il dipinto costa mille dollari.	The painting costs one thousand dollars.
Cento anni fa...	One hundred years ago...
Mille anni fa...	One thousand years ago...
Un migliaio...	About a thousand...
Migliaia di persone guardano il calcio.	Thousands of people watch soccer.

Chapter 8 – Getting Ready

Practice – 20

Numbers – Counting 1 million-10 million by millions

Un milione	One million
Due milioni	Two million
Tre milioni	Three million
Quattro milioni	Four million
Cinque milioni	Five million
Sei milioni	Six million
Sette milioni	Seven million
Otto milioni	Eight million
Nove milioni	Nine million
Dieci milioni	Ten million

Practice – 21

Numbers – Counting 1 billion-5 billion by billions

Un miliardo	One billion
Due miliardi	Two billion
Tre miliardi	Three billion
Quattro miliardi	Four billion
Cinque miliardi	Five billion

Practice – 22

Numbers – **Di** with **milione/milioni** and **miliardo/miliardi** before a noun

Ci sono un milione di persone a Napoli.	There are a million people in Naples.
Ci sono due milioni settecentomila persone a Roma.	There are two million seven hundred thousand people in Rome.
Ci sono più di un miliardo di persone in Cina.	There are more than a billion people in China.
Ci sono due miliardi di dollari in banca.	There are two billion dollars in the bank.

Milan
Duomo at Sunset

Chapter 9 – It's a Party!

Practice – 1

Important Phrases – Meeting and greeting at a gathering – Welcoming phrases

Benvenuto!	Welcome! (to a male)
Benvenuta!	Welcome! (to a female)
Benvenuti!	Welcome! (to a group of males or a group of males and females)
Benvenute!	Welcome! (to a group of females)
Entri!	Come in! (polite command)
Entra!	Come in! (familiar command)
Si accomodi!	Make yourself comfortable. (polite command)
Accomodati!	Make yourself comfortable! (familiar command)
Si sieda!	Sit down. (polite command)
Siediti!	Sit down! (familiar command)
Da questa parte, prego.	This way, if you please.

Practice – 2

Important Phrases – Meeting and greeting at a gathering – Introductions

Ti presento il signor Bianco.	(I) introduce you to Mr. White.
Piacere di conoscerla.	Pleased to meet you. (polite)
Piacere di conoscerti.	Pleased to meet you. (familiar)
Lieto(a) di conoscerla.	Delighted to meet you. (male/female speaker polite)
Lieto(a) di conoscerti.	Delighted to meet you. (male/female speaker familiar)
Molto lieto! / Molto lieta!	Delighted! (male/female speaker)
Piacere mio!	The pleasure is mine!
Sono molto contento(a) di vederti!	(I) am very happy to see you! (male/ female speaker familiar)
Sono molto contento(a) di vederla!	(I) am very happy to see you! (male/ female speaker polite)
Sono molto contento(a) di rivederti!	(I) am very happy to see you again! (male/female speaker familiar)
Sono molto contento(a) di rivederla!	(I) am very happy to see you again! (male/female speaker polite)

Chapter 9 – It's a Party!

Practice – 3

Important Phrases – Meeting and greeting at a gathering – Breaking the ice

Si ricorda di me?	Do you remember me? (polite)
È di questa zona?	Are you from around here? (polite)
Sei di queste parti?	Are you from around here? (familiar)
Di che cosa si occupa?	What do you do?
Mi occupo di affari.	I'm in business.
Sono studente. / Sono studentessa.	I'm a student. (male/female speaker)
Che lavoro fai?	What do you do?
Sono in affari.	I am in business.
Non mi dica!	You don't say!
Sono contento per lei. / Sono contenta per lei.	I am happy for you. (male/female speaker) (polite)
Sono contento per te. / Sono contenta per te.	I am happy for you. (male/female speaker) (familiar)
Mi piace tanto!	I love it! I like it so much! (lit. It is very pleasing to me!)
Mi piace un sacco!	I love it! (idiomatic expression)

Practice – 4

Important Phrases – Meeting and greeting at a gathering – Departing

Devo andare via ora.	I must go (leave) now.
Ti sei divertito?	(Did) you enjoy yourself? (to a male)
Ti sei divertita?	(Did) you enjoy yourself? (to a female)
È stato un piacere.	It has been a pleasure.
È stato divertente.	It has been fun.
Mi sono proprio divertito.	I really enjoyed myself / had a great time. (male speaker)
Mi sono proprio divertita.	I really enjoyed myself / had a great time. (female speaker)
Grazie di tutto.	Thanks for everything.
Grazie per la tua ospitalità.	Thank you for your hospitality. (familiar)
Grazie per una bella serata.	Thank you for a nice/beautiful evening.
Ti ringrazio.	I thank you. (familiar)
La ringrazio.	I thank you. (polite)

Chapter 9 – It's a Party!

Practice – 5

Titles and proper forms of address / Use of **il, dal,** and **di** with professions

Signore	Sir or gentleman
Signora	Madam or lady/gentlewoman
Signore e signori	Ladies and gentlemen
Il Signore	The Lord (refers to God)
Un signore	A lord
Una signora	A lady
Signori e signore	Lords and ladies
Il signor Rossi	Mr. Rossi
La signora Rossi	Mrs. Rossi
Il signor Rossi è un ingegnere.	Mr. Rossi is an engineer.
Io sono ingegnere.	I am (an) engineer.
Paolo è medico.	Paul is (a) medical doctor.
Vado dal dottore.	I go to the doctor.
Vorrei parlare con il dottore.	I would like to speak with the doctor.
Il signor Rossi non è alla festa stasera.	Mr. Rossi is not at the party tonight.

Practice – 6

Che and **cui** for who and whom / Use of definite article with **cui** for whose

La ragazza che viaggia è Caterina.	The girl who travels is Kathy.
La macchina che Pietro guida è rossa.	The car that Peter drives is red.
La persona con cui viaggiamo è Caterina.	The person with whom we travel is Kathy.
Il cugino di cui io parlo è Pietro.	The cousin about whom I speak is Peter.
Il cugino a cui io scrivo è Pietro.	The cousin to whom I write is Peter.
Ecco Caterina, il cui cugino è Pietro.	Here is Kathy, whose cousin is Peter.
Ti presento Caterina, la cui famiglia è in America.	I introduce to you Kathy, whose family is in America.

Chapter 9 – It's a Party!

Practice – 7

Comprare – present tense (begins with consonant) **– compro**

Use of direct object pronouns **lo, la, li,** and **le** before **compro** to replace nouns

Vocabulary – Making yourself comfortable at home

Io compro il cuscino.	I buy the pillow.
Lo compro.	(I) buy it.

Io compro la lampada.	I buy the lamp.
La compro.	(I) buy it.

Io compro lo specchio.	I buy the mirror.
Lo compro.	(I) buy it.

Io compro l'asciugamano.	I buy the towel.
Lo compro.	(I) buy it.

Io compro i cuscini.	I buy the pillows.
Li compro.	(I) buy them.

Io compro le lampade.	I buy the lamps.
Le compro.	(I) buy them.

Io compro gli specchi.	I buy the mirrors.
Li compro.	(I) buy them.

Io compro gli asciugamani.	I buy the towels.
Li compro.	(I) buy them.

Chapter 9 – It's a Party!

Practice – 8

Comprare – present tense (begins with consonant) **– compro, compri, compra**

Use of direct object pronouns **lo, la, li,** and **le** before **comprare** to replace nouns

Vocabulary – Making yourself comfortable at home

Io compro il cuscino.	I buy the pillow.
Lo compro.	(I) buy it.

Tu compri la lampada.	You buy the lamp.
La compri.	(You) buy it.

Caterina compra lo specchio.	Kathy buys the mirror.
Caterina lo compra.	Kathy buys it.

Pietro compra l'asciugamano.	Peter buys the towel.
Pietro lo compra.	Peter buys it.

Io compro i cuscini.	I buy the pillows.
Li compro.	(I) buy them.

Tu compri le lampade.	You buy the lamps.
Le compri.	(You) buy them.

Caterina compra gli specchi.	Kathy buys the mirrors.
Caterina li compra.	Kathy buys them.

Pietro compra gli asciugamani.	Peter buys the towels.
Pietro li compra.	Peter buys them.

Chapter 9 – It's a Party!

Practice – 9

Ordinare – present tense (begins with vowel) **– ordino, ordini, ordina**

Use of direct object pronouns **l', li,** and **le** before **ordinare** to replace nouns

Vocabulary – Making yourself comfortable at home

Io ordino il cuscino.	I order the pillow.
L'ordino.	(I) order it.

Tu ordini la lampada.	You order the lamp.
L'ordini.	(You) order it.

Caterina ordina lo specchio.	Kathy orders the mirror.
Caterina l'ordina.	Kathy orders it.

Pietro ordina l'asciugamano.	Peter orders the towel.
Pietro l'ordina.	Peter orders it.

Io ordino i cuscini.	I order the pillows.
Li ordino.	(I) order them.

Tu ordini le lampade.	You order the lamps.
Le ordini.	(You) order them.

Caterina ordina gli specchi.	Kathy orders the mirrors.
Caterina li ordina.	Kathy orders them.

Pietro ordina gli asciugamani.	Peter orders the towels.
Pietro li ordina.	Peter orders them.

Chapter 9 – It's a Party!

Practice – 10

Amare – present tense (begins with vowel) **– amo, ami, ama**

Use of direct object pronoun **l'** before **amare** to replace persons

Michele ama la sua fidanzata.	Micheal loves his girlfriend.
Michele l'ama.	Michael loves her.

Caterina ama il suo fidanzato.	Kathy loves her boyfriend.
Caterina l'ama.	Kathy loves him.

Mio padre ama mia madre.	My father loves my mother.
Mio padre l'ama.	My father loves her.

Mia madre ama mio padre.	My mother loves my father.
Mia madre l'ama.	My mother loves him.

Practice – 11

Amare – present tense (begins with vowel) **– amo, ami, ama**

Use of direct object pronoun **l'** before **amare** to replace persons, with negative

Michele non ama più la sua fidanzata.	Micheal doesn't love his girlfriend anymore.
Michele non l'ama.	Michael doesn't love her.

Caterina non ama più il suo fidanzato.	Kathy doesn't love her boyfriend anymore.
Caterina non l'ama.	Kathy doesn't love him.

Chapter 9 – It's a Party!

Practice – 12

Familiar commands for **"are"** verbs:

Guardare – imperative tense **– Guarda! Guardiamo! Guardate!**

Aspettare – imperative tense **– Aspetta! Aspettiamo! Aspettate!**

Aiutare – imperative tense **– Aiuta! Aiutiamo! Aiutate!**

Andare – imperative tense (irreg.) **– Và! Andiamo! Andate!**

Use of direct object pronouns with the imperative

Guarda!	Look!
Guardami!	Look at me!
Guardiamo!	Let's look!
Guardate!	You all look!
Guardatemi!	You all look at me!

Aspetta!	Wait!
Aspettami!	Wait for me!
Aspettiamo!	Let's wait!
Aspettate!	You all wait!
Aspettatemi!	You all wait for me!

Aiuta!	Help!
Aiutami!	Help me!
Aiutiamo!	Let's help!
Aiutate!	You all help!
Aiutatemi!	You all help me!

Và! (= Vai)	Go!
Vai via!	Go away!
Andiamo!	Let's go!
Andate!	You all go!

Chapter 9 – It's a Party!

Practice – 13

Familiar commands for **"are"** and **"ere"** reflexive verbs:

Sbrigarsi – imperative tense reflexive **– Sbrigati! Sbrighiamoci! Sbrigatevi!**

Muoversi – imperative tense reflexive **– Muoviti! Muoviamoci! Muovetevi!**

Dai!– imperative expression

Sbrigati!	Hurry (yourself) up!
Sbrighiamoci!	Let's hurry (ourselves) up!
Sbrigatevi!	You all hurry (yourselves) up!
Dai!	Come on!

Muoviti!	Move yourself!
Muoviamoci!	Let's move ourselves!
Muovetevi!	You all move yourselves!

Practice – 14

Avere – imperative tense (irreg.) **– Abbi! Abbiamo! Abbiate!**

Essere – imperative tense (irreg.) **– Sii! Siamo! Siate!**

Stare – imperative tense (irreg.) **– Stà! Stai! Stiamo! State!**

Abbi pazienza!	Have patience!
Abbiamo pazienza!	Let's have patience!
Abbiate pazienza!	You all have patience!

Sii bravo!	Be good!
Siamo bravi!	Let's be good!
Siate bravi!	You all be good!

Sta' bene! (= Stai)	Be well!
Stai bene!	Be well!
Stiamo bene!	Let's stay well!
State bene!	You all be well!

Chapter 9 – It's a Party!

Practice – 15

Familiar commands for **"ere"** verbs:

Rispondere – imperative tense **– Rispondi! Rispondiamo! Rispondete!**

Correre – imperative tense **– Corri! Corriamo! Correte!**

Prendere – imperative tense **– Prendi! Prendiamo! Prendete!**

Scendere – imperative tense **– Scendi! Scendiamo! Scendete!**

Use of direct object pronouns with the imperative

Rispondi!	Answer!
Rispondimi!	Answer me!
Rispondiamo!	Let's answer!
Rispondete!	You all answer!

Corri!	Run!
Corriamo!	Let's run!
Correte!	You all run!

Prendi!	Take!
Prendilo!	Take it!
Prendiamo!	Let's take it!
Prendetelo!	You all take it!

Scendi!	Get off! / Get down!
Scendiamo!	Let's get off! / Let's get down!
Scendete!	You all get off! / You all get down!

Chapter 9 – It's a Party!

Practice – 16

Familiar commands for **"ere"** verbs:

Partire – imperative tense **– Parti! Partiamo! Partite!**

Finire – imperative tense (irreg.) **– Finisci! Finiamo! Finite!**

Salire – imperative tense (irreg.) **– Sali! Saliamo! Salite!**

Uscire – imperative tense (irreg.) **– Esci! Usciamo! Uscite!**

Venire – imperative tense (irreg.) **– Vieni! Veniamo! Venite!**

Parti!	Leave!
Partiamo!	Let's leave!
Partite!	You all leave!

Finisci!	Finish!
Finiamo!	Let's finish!
Finite!	You all finish!

Sali!	Get in!
Saliamo!	Let's get in!
Salite!	You all get in!

Esci!	Get out!
Usciamo!	Let's get out!
Uscite!	You all get out!

Vieni qua!	Come here!
Veniamo!	Let's come!
Venite qua!	You all come here!

Chapter 9 – It's a Party!

Practice – 17

Familiar commands for important irregular verbs:

Dare – imperative tense (irreg.) **– Dà! Diamo! Date!**

Dire – imperative tense (irreg.) **– Dì! Diciamo! Dite!**

Fare – imperative tense (irreg.) **– Fà! Facciamo! Fate!**

Use of direct object pronouns with the imperative – irregular forms

Dà! (Dai!)	Give!
Dammi!	Give me!
Dammi una mano!	Give me a hand!
Dammelo!	Give it to me!
Diamo...!	Let's give...!
Date...!	You all give...!
Datemi!	You all give me!
Datemelo!	You all give it to me!

Dì! (Dici!)	Speak!
Dimmi!	Speak to me!
Diciamo!	Let's talk! / Let's say...
Dite!	You all, speak!
Ditemi!	You all, speak to me!

Fà! (Fai!)	Do...!
Fallo!	Do it!
Facciamolo!	Let's do it!
Fate...!	You all do...!
Fatelo!	You all do it!

Chapter 9 – It's a Party!

Practice – 18

Parlare – negative imperative **– Non parlare! Non parliamo! Non parlate!**

Preoccuparsi – negative reflexive imperative **– Non preoccuparti!**

Use of direct object pronouns with **preoccuparsi**

Non parlare!	Don't talk! (you familiar)
Non preoccuparti!	Don't worry yourself! (you familiar)
Non parliamo!	Let's not talk!
Non parlate!	You all don't talk!

Practice – 19

Idiomatic expressions, **"Dare del tu"** and **"Dare del Lei"**

Dare – do, dai, dà, diamo / Usare – usa

Mi può dare del tu.	You can use the familiar form of "you" with me. (polite)
Mi puoi dare del tu!	You can use the familiar form of "you" with me! (familiar command)
Le posso dare del tu?	Can I use the familiar form of "you" with you? (polite)

Diamoci del tu!	Let's use the familiar form of "you" with each other!
Dammi del tu!	Use the familiar form of "you" with me! (familiar command)

Mi dia del Lei, per favore!	Use the polite form of "you" with me, please! (polite command)
Io do del Lei al padrone.	I use the polite form of "you" with the owner.
Tu dai del Lei al tuo capo.	You use the polite form of "you" with your boss.
Lui dà del Lei al prete.	He uses the polite form of "you" with the priest.
Lei usa il Lei con il prete.	She uses the polite form of "you" with the priest.

Chapter 9 – It's a Party!

Practice – 20

Numbers – The date in Italian by decades, with years of special significance for the author

Millenovecento	1900
Millenovecentodieci	1910
Millenovecentoventi	1920
Millenovecentotrenta	1930
Millenovecentoquaranta	1940
Millenovecentocinquanta	1950
Millenovecentosessanta	1960
Millenovecentosessantadue	1962
Millenovecentosettanta	1970
Millenovecentottanta	1980
Millenovecentonovanta	1990
Millenovecentonovantasei	1996

Duemila	2000
Duemilauno	2001
Duemiladieci	2010
Duemiladodici	2012

Practice – 21

Numbers – References to decades and centuries

Gli anni sessanta	the 60s (lit. the years 60, usually a reference to the 1960s)
Gli anni dell'ottocento	the 1800s (lit. the years 800, usually a reference to the 19th century)
Gli anni del cinquecento	the 1500s (lit. the years 500, usually a reference to the 16th century)